The Geography of Nowhere

Finding One's Self in the Postmodern World

Gary Eberle

Sheed & Ward

Copyright© 1994 by Gary Eberle

Sheed & Ward™ is a service of The National Catholic Reporter Publishing Company.

Library of Congress Cataloguing-in-Publication Data

Eberle, Gary
    The geography of nowhere : finding one's self in the postmodern world / Gary Eberle.
        p. cm.
    Includes bibliographical references and index.
    ISBN 1-55612-716-2 (alk. paper)
    1. Spiritual life. 2. Postmodernism—Religious aspects.
I. Title.
BL624.E22   1994
291.4—dc20   94-19420
                                              CIP

Published by: Sheed & Ward
                   115 E. Armour Blvd.
                   P.O. Box 419492
                   Kansas City, MO 64141

To order, call: (800) 333-7373

Cover design Copyright© 1994 by Emil Antonucci.

Contents

To Sue

Introduction

IT IS THE ASSUMPTION OF THIS BOOK THAT MOST PEOPLE IN history have been able to locate themselves in some meaningful way in time and place. Through sacred histories, mythologies, and attachment to a sort of spiritual geography which overlaid (or undergirded) the physical geography of their world, humans of past generations were able, almost without reflection, to tell you where they were at any given moment.

By our modern standards of cartography, of course, they were often "wrong" about where they thought they were, but however inaccurate their mapmaking, they carried about in their heads a definite sense of how the world was put together, and that sense must have offered them a comfort and sense of belonging that few people in the contemporary world seem to feel.

For, despite our current ability to pinpoint ourselves on a geophysical map with the aid of satellites and other technologies, and in spite of the fact that we have explored and charted virtually every inch of the globe on which we live and the galaxy which we inhabit, there remains among many of our finest and brightest minds a sense of being lost, adrift in a cosmos whose reliable points of reference—God, church, society, sense of self—have either sunk below the horizon or have broken loose and are themselves randomly afloat.

If we're honest, we all must feel a sense of anomie and disjunction if and when we take time to think about life in the modern world. We have even grown used to this feeling, so much so that it often strikes us as odd when anyone suggests that there may be other, less chaotic ways to live.

We live in a geography of nowhere. Unconnected bits and pieces of a vast, complex world pass by us constantly in the form of televised sound bites filled with news from places we've never heard of, ads selling us things we never asked to have, pop entertainment shaping our values, radio, newspapers and magazines filling us with undigested information twenty-four hours a day.

We have grown alienated from the places in which we live. While appearing to "know" intimate details of the lives of the popes, presidents and third world dictators who come into our living rooms daily, we may remain totally ignorant of our neighbors a few houses down the street. We may be more aware and more deeply moved by the plight of starving masses in Africa than we are of the street people in our own downtowns. We live in a "dystopia," a state of being and of mind which many feel is horribly disjointed, where even the most fortunate may often feel they are living meagre, wretched and fearful lives, impoverished in spirit and even unconscious of their own despair.

If we regard this bleak, fragmented world as an end point, there seems to be room for little but pessimism. Things go from bad to worse and historical processes are irreversible. So it goes. If, however, we see it as merely a phase in human development, a period of necessary disintegration before a new reconstruction, then some optimism may be salvaged. I believe that history favors those who look for connections rather than divisions, and it is the intention of this book to draw some disparate things together in what amounts to a personal synthesis that, I hope, others may benefit from.

In an age of increasing specialization this book is intentionally generalist in its approach, hearkening back, I hope, to a time in our Western tradition before poetry, science and religion—not to mention psychology—were fragmented from each other, and when all areas of mental inquiry were carried on under the umbrella of Natural Philosophy. In those days, anyone, regardless of academic specialty, could join in the conversation.

Inevitably, this generalist approach will lose in detail what it is attempting to gain in scope. In an essay that tries to discern a general pattern in such diverse fields as literature, philosophy, physics, anthropology, psychology and comparative mythology, there will no doubt be some oversimplification, but I feel confident that once the general argument of the book is granted, the pieces will fall into place in the readers' minds, whatever their own expertise.

We live in an age of exploding information and most people feel overwhelmed by it. We have been taught that things will become clear when we have all the information available, but today no one can possibly absorb all the information that is out there. The problem, obviously, is not that we lack information, but that we lack a *pattern* which will make sense of the increasing amounts of it which are constantly raining down on us like confetti.

With so much information, the process of assembling it into some sort of order must be somewhat serendipitous. Like our paleolithic ancestors, we modern hunter-gatherers must wander through the geography of nowhere picking up bits and pieces of worldviews that we may find useful; we must try to patch together a meaningful life for ourselves from these fragments. Having too much information to absorb, we may sometimes feel as though we have nothing at all, but we often uncover useful things while on our way to someplace else. We stumble upon meaningful fragments with which we piece together a mosaic. We see the pattern only when we step back.

The connections among the pieces which follow may be as poetic as they are rational, and some of the ideas presented here may require the sorts of metaphoric leaps one makes readily when reading verse, and yet, this is how one makes one's way in the geography of nowhere. Like early explorers setting out for unknown regions, we must bring optimism with us, as well as the hope that what lies out there beyond the horizon of nowhere will be a brand new world full of wonder.

NOTE: Though this book was originally written to be read as a unified essay, it may also be useful in the classroom to introduce students to the problems of spirituality in the postmodern world or in the context of courses on personal development. To that end, some critical apparatus such as a Glossary, Index, and Suggestions for Further Discussion and Reflection as well as Suggested Readings have been added at the end of the text. Individuals may wish to use the Suggestions for Further Reflection to continue their own thinking about ideas and issues presented in the text. Words that appear in the Glossary are asterisked (*) at their first appearance in the text.

CHAPTER 1

The Geography of Nowhere

SUPPOSE TIME TRAVEL WERE POSSIBLE, AND SUPPOSE THAT YOU could invite a person from the not-too-distant past to visit your home. Let's say our time traveller lived only 150 years ago, in the mid-part of the nineteenth century, and our time machine is able to pluck him from his own time and place and bring him magically to ours.

Assuming that the trip alone did not kill him, our time tourist would still have an extremely difficult time getting comfortable once our machine had deposited him in the midst of what we call normal daily life. He would scarcely be able to make head or tail of what we refer to as our "lifestyle."

Nothing about it would seem "normal" to him at all. Though separated from us by only three or four generations, our visitor would find the simplest detail of our daily routine baffling. To heat water for morning tea, for example, no fire is necessary. We simply arise, stumble into the kitchen and put our coffee mugs into a strange metal box, push some buttons that beep and pop and, after some whirring noise, we remove a cup of hot water from the microwave. Everything is cooked in this device in a matter of only a few minutes, if not seconds. Modern kitchens are not hot, smokey or greasy. There may not even be evidence of fire—that constant companion of the human species since its domestication some half a million years ago.

Even if the family our guest is visiting is not particularly affluent, our time traveller would still be astounded by the number of *things* the family owns. Hundreds of things, large and small, fill every nook and cranny of their house. The visitor doesn't know the names of many of these things nor can he even guess their uses. Many of these things are hardly ever used by his hosts, but they are there nonetheless, an impressive array of material goods, virtually all of which are made from some form of plastic, a substance which, to our traveller, is both like and unlike wood, metal or fiber. The colors strike him as bright and unearthly.

When nighttime comes, the family's activities do not slow down. As the sun descends over the horizon, electric lights come on so that work, play and social interchange continue unabated. This family, indeed, seems to live in perpetual light, taking no heed of the natural transitions from day to night and back again.

Most of all, our time traveller might be totally bewildered by how dislocated this life is. The people spend so much of their lives connected electronically to someplace else that most of the time they hardly seem to be *there*, or anywhere at all, for that matter.

On a typical evening in this typical American home, our time traveller sometimes feels alone even though he is surrounded by people. The father sits in front of the television set watching a news broadcast live from the other side of the globe. Mother is in the kitchen talking on the telephone to her sister who lives in Milwaukee, several hundred miles away. As she talks, she listens to music by the eighteenth century Italian composer Vivaldi courtesy of the radio station at the local university some 50 miles away. The children are off in their rooms, also alone. Brother is watching a British rock group on MTV on his own television set while his sister is plugged into a computer communicating through her keyboard with remote parts of the city, country or world. None of them seems to pay much attention to the people in the immediate surroundings.

Life in the modern world, as perceived by our time traveller, must seem scattershot. Nothing feels related to any center. It seems, by comparison with his own time, to lack coherence. In fact, there is little about the house and its neighborhood that would even give our traveller an idea of where exactly in the world he is.

The television sets, radios and stereo equipment in the home were made in Japan. The clothing the family wears was made in Sri Lanka, India, Jamaica. Their shoes come from Taiwan. In the kitchen they have French wine, German beer, and coffee grown in the mountains of Colombia. Virtually nothing comes from the state or region they actually live in. Except for the fact that American English is spoken in the home, he could as well be in Japan, Germany or almost anywhere else in the "civilized" world.

At first, the sensory overload would be tremendous. Our time traveller would be suffering from total culture shock. Those of us who have travelled outside our own cultures can only imagine how dislocated he is. Where—indeed *how*—could he possibly locate himself? If he had lived in one of the new industrial towns of the mid-1800's, he might have some cues to guide him, but otherwise there is little in this modern domestic environment that he can identify. Virtually nothing is the same as it was only 150 years ago.

If he had travelled some 150 years in the *other* direction, into his past, to the year 1700, there would not have been nearly as vast a difference in the way people lived. The rhythms of hearth and home would have been immediately recognized.

If life *inside* the home is confounding to him, imagine our tourist's surprise—amazement, astonishment even—as he leaves the relatively serene atmosphere of the modern home and heads *out* into the fast lane of a typical suburban area. His host family lives—as do most contemporary Americans—in what journalist Joel Garreau has called an "Edge City,"* one of those new towns that have sprung up in the past thirty years, almost by accident, it seems, around the fringes of most American—and most modern—cities as the automobile has increased its hegemony over modern life. Edge cities grow up around freeway interchanges, for the most part, and their most distinctive feature is that they have no center, at least not in the sense that urban areas have had "centers" ever since human beings began living in permanent settlements in the Middle East some 5,000 years ago.

It is a life that is oddly dislocated from anything our traveller would identify as "real."

The subdivision the family lives in may be called Sherwood Forest or Glenwood Cove, but there is no forest, wood, glen or cove nearby. The streets, with their quaint, vaguely countrified names, seem to meander with no particular point, ending often in cul-de-sacs. The street names may attempt to connect the neighborhood with

---

*See Appendix I: Glossary.

something historical, "Appian Way" or "Trapper's Creek Road," but there is little sense of history about the area. Everything appears to have dropped from the sky at one time and our visitor does not feel the pressure of layers of the past that he might have felt elsewhere.

For getting around, this twentieth-century family seems utterly dependent on its personal transportation vehicle, affectionately called the car. They take it everywhere. They seem unwilling to walk more than 600 feet in any direction before they will take a car instead. This car runs on gasoline refined from petroleum taken from the ground in the Middle East. It is an expensive way to travel and a great deal of the family's time and money goes into maintaining its several vehicles. The family explains to him that they must have more than one because they all head in different directions at all hours of the day and night, going to work, to school, to church and other activities.

As our time traveller leaves the host family's cul-de-sac and heads into the nearby commercial strip at 50 or 60 miles an hour, his eyes are dazzled by the bright signs. He is amazed at how many of the establishments along the route depend on the automobile for their existence. Not only the obvious ones—the car lots, the muffler shops—but virtually every business along the strip depends on the automobile and its ability to move individuals fast.

The host pulls into a strip mall to visit a store where he can have his shoes repaired, then drives another couple of miles to buy a few nails and some lumber for a deck he is building, then a few more miles to buy clothing. None of the clerks at any of the stores seems to know him. Their interchanges are strictly business. In some cases, the host does not even have to deal with human beings at all. He goes to a bank, inserts a card, pushes a few buttons and, miracle of miracles, money comes out of the wall!

In the mornings, the children are driven by the mother several miles to a large school that looks from the distance like a prison or factory. Father goes in the opposite direction, to work in the old core city. Mother has a job in an adjoining suburb. In the evening, children, parents and neighbors all head for different destinations, all of which seem to lie in places quite distant from where the family lives—or, more correctly, sleeps. For it soon becomes apparent to our time-travelling guest that except for those few hours each night when the lights and the televisions and computers are turned off, this family spends very little time "living" in any sense that he might understand the word.

After some time, let's say a few weeks, he notices that his initial sense of unease has not abated. He'd originally attributed it to what his hosts helpfully called "jet lag." "You'll get used to it," they told him in the early stages of his visit as they popped in and out of doors, raced off in all directions, ate at odd hours and always kept one eye, it seemed, on the box they called the TV.

But as the weeks went on, he did not grow used to it. If anything, he grew more disoriented. He wanted to stop his hosts' mad rushing about and talk with them about this, but they seemed always too busy. Once, when he was caught staring thoughtfully out the window, his hostess asked him, "Are you all right?"

"Oh, yes," he'd replied, "I was just thinking."

A look of concern came over her face then.

"Are you *sure* you're all right?"

"I was just taking a moment to try to think," he might say. It seemed to him that back home, back in the previous century, there had been more time to think. If anything, there had been too much time. Here, by comparison, time seemed to be a precious commodity. People were endlessly talking about trying to "save" it.

He would have said something about this, but he had been in this time and place long enough to know that if he voiced any concerns, his helpful host or hostess might reply, "If you're depressed or anything, we can get a prescription for you."

Well, that's about enough. Let us follow our time traveller as he—gratefully, we may suppose—flies back to his own time and place.

The first thing he must notice, on his return, is the silence. No humming of TV's, radios, or computers, no din of automobiles, no telephones ringing to interrupt his thoughts. Perhaps, if he lives in a city, the clatter of horse hooves intrudes once in a while, but it is a quite different rhythm.

In reflecting on his trip to the future, he can summon up only fragments which refuse to organize themselves into any meaningful pattern. Indeed, if someone asks him where he's been, he may well reply, "I'm not sure" because he has come home without any real sense of having been anyplace at all. He may, in fact, say—as Gertrude Stein was reputed to have said of Los Angeles—"There is no *there* there," and, indeed, he may be correct.

As communications theorist Joshua Meyrowitz has pointed out in his book *No Sense of Place: The Impact of Electronic Media on Social Behavior,*[1] those of us living in this contemporary "mediated" world have little or no sense of either a physical place or social place to which we belong. We are living lives without geographic or, by extension, moral and spiritual centers. Most of us cannot really locate ourselves in space or time in any meaningful sense of the words. We find ourselves living in a geography of nowhere.

The Modern World

How did this strange state of affairs come about?

If we traverse the distance that our time traveller came more slowly, we might get some idea. Between his time and ours, in the space of only four or five generations, more changes have occurred in the way we live our day to day lives than occurred in the previous two millenia. The pace and the scope of the change have been astounding, outstripping our ability even to make sense of them. Alvin Toffler coined the term "future shock" back in the early 1970's to describe this state of affairs, but, if anything, the shock has only grown more profound since then. The acceleration and overload actually began some time ago but only became critical in fairly recent times.

Between 1880 and 1910, in the space of less than half of a single lifetime, all the significant pieces of modern* life burst onto the world stage. In historical terms, the effects were almost as instantaneous as they were far-reaching. The telephone, telegraph and radio shrank distances and speeded up communications. Harnessing electricity gave us a new source of power and, more importantly, light

---

[1] Joshua Meyrowitz, *No Sense of Place: The Impact of Electronic Media on Social Behavior*. New York: Oxford Univ. Press, 1984.

which forever banished the night as it had been experienced for millenia. In medicine, the discovery of germ theory and X-rays revolutionized diagnosis and cure. Nearly every device on which so much of our normal daily routine depends (except the computer) was invented during that remarkable period. Airplanes, moving pictures, the phonograph, and the automobile all came to be around the turn of this century. Even television, the device that has shaped the latter half of this century more than any other, had its theoretical foundations laid during this time period.

The Western* world entered this century with unbounded hope. Coming at the end of two hundred years of scientific triumph, there was nearly unlimited optimism. The idea of Progress* was elevated to the status of theology, and "progress," inevitably, was defined in scientific and technical terms. J. B. Bury, in *The Idea of Progress: An Inquiry into its Origin and Growth*, wrote of this mood of optimism that imbued the end of the last century. His (to us) hyperbolic language is typical of sort of effusions written at the time:

> Since [the Great] Exhibition [of 1851], western civilization has advanced steadily . . . . The most striking advance has been in the technical conveniences of life—that is, in the control over natural forces. It would be superfluous to enumerate the discoveries and inventions since 1850 which have abridged space, economized time, eased bodily suffering, and reduced in some ways the friction of life, though they have increased it in others. This uninterrupted series of technical inventions, proceeding concurrently with immense enlargements of all branches of knowledge, has gradually accustomed the least speculative mind to the conception that civilisation is naturally progressive, and that continuous improvement is part of the order of things.[2]

Bury quotes the Victorian sociologist Herbert Spencer to the effect that this modern world is progressing toward utopia:

> "Always towards perfection is the mighty movement—towards a complete development and a more unmixed good; subordinating in

---

[2]J. B. Bury, *The Idea of Progress: An Inquiry into its Origin and Growth*. New York: Dover Publications, 1955. p. 332.

its universality all petty irregularities and fallings back, as the curvature of the earth subordinates mountains and valleys."[3]

Progress was a natural force, wiping out all evils—disease, poverty, war, perhaps even death itself—in its triumph.

Of course, from our less optimistic perspective at the end of the twentieth century, these ideas seem rather naive, but how could those living at what seemed such an epochal moment of human history have foreseen the horrors that their emerging science would unleash?

And unleash them, it did. Though there were some cracks in the edifice even at the turn of the century, it was the First World War that delivered the death blow to the optimism of the young century. That war demonstrated that the same technology that promised to solve so many of mankind's problems and fulfill so many of our dreams could also provide new methods of mechanized mass destruction. The machine gun, poison gas, aerial bombs, tanks—all these weapons of mass destruction were developed, their full implications unseen, during the age of optimism that preceded the war.

Believing that the conflict, which began in August, 1914, would be over by Christmas, the British set off, anticipating a sort of glorious adventure. Charging in straight lines, as they had successfully done for a couple of hundred years, they thought they were fighting an old fashioned war. The Germans, who had the foresight to realize they were living in a new century which demanded a new style of warfare, simply mowed them down with their machine guns. Tens of thousands died in single battles. The hostilities degenerated into a bloody war of attrition in which the horrors of modern mass slaughter, poison gas and aerial bombing succeeded in wiping out an entire generation of young men. By the time the war ended in 1919, nearly 38 million were dead or wounded on all sides and the optimistic illusion of a glorious future through science was shattered forever.

And so was the old faith in eternal verities that had sustained generations past.

The post-war writers were the first to pick up on it.

W. B. Yeats, in his famous "The Second Coming" (1919) wrote of a world in which

---

[3]Ibid., p. 340.

> Things fall apart; the center cannot hold;
> Mere anarchy is loosed upon the world,
> The blood-dimmed tide is loosed and everywhere
> The ceremony of innocence is drowned.[4]

In Yeats' vision, the terrible omens of the first World War presaged a bestial age about to be born, a 2000-year cycle of blood and destruction to be presided over by some rough beast then slouching its way to Bethlehem to be born.

T. S. Eliot in *The Waste Land* (1925) painted the picture of a world in disarray where language degenerated sometimes to mere gibberish, and the long tradition of what was known as "Western Civilization" seemed at an end. Nothing in this new world was connected to anything else and the poem leaves us with an image of the wounded Fisher King from *Parzival* probing the depths as the culture of Western Europe collapses around him in a Babel of fragments of a half-remembered past.

Similarly, Hemingway, in *A Farewell to Arms* (1929), articulated his generation's lost faith in the old abstract ideas that had formed the very fiber of the civilization that had just inflicted such carnage on itself.

> I did not say anything. I was always embarrassed by the words sacred, glorious, and sacrifice and the expression in vain. We had heard them, sometimes standing in the rain almost out of earshot so that only the shouted words came through, and had read them, on proclamations, now for a long time, and I had seen nothing sacred, and the things that were glorious had no glory and the sacrifices were like the stockyards at Chicago if nothing was done with the meat except bury it. There were many words that you could not stand to hear and finally only the names of places had dignity. Certain numbers were the same way and certain dates and these with the names of the places were all you could say and have them mean anything. Abstract words such as glory, honor, courage or hallow were obscene beside the concrete names of villages, the numbers of the roads, the names of the rivers, the numbers of regiments and the dates.[5]

---

[4]W. B. Yeats, *Selected Poems and Two Plays of William Butler Yeats*, M. L. Rosenthal, ed. New York: Macmillan, 1962.

To the writers and intellectuals between the wars, the world before the war seemed separated from the brave new post-war world by a wide chasm and we "modern" human beings were left standing in a waste land, bereft of the values that had allowed our predecessors to pull themselves up out of despair.

Civilization and Its Discontents

It was not the First World War alone, of course, that caused such a profound rift with the past. The carnage of the war had simply manured the ground and thus fertilized the seeds of despair and pessimism which had already been planted in the nineteenth century. The fabric of what had been "Western Civilization" was already fraying as the century turned, though few of the optimists realized it.

Throughout the Victorian period, as the breach between science and religion widened, and as an increasingly secular materialist culture* finally displaced the last vestiges of medievalism, a new view of the human species and its relationship to the universe around it had been emerging.

In 1859, Charles Darwin had published his epochal *On the Origin of Species* which proposed, for the first time, a mechanism (Natural Selection) by which one species may evolve into another. The implications of his thesis on the theological worldview of the West were evident from the outset and the shock waves can still be felt. If human beings, as Darwin stated, were indeed evolved from "lower" forms of life, then what happens to mankind's exalted view of itself as a special creation, a linchpin, as it were, in God's universal plan?

Humankind's traditional place atop the animal universe was shaken, but what of the inner universe, that place within us, traditionally called the soul, where animal met the divine? That, too, received a shock.

At the turn of the century, in Vienna, Freud was conducting the self-analysis which would yield his famous psychoanalytic theory* which, more than any other model of the mind propounded in our time, has shaped the way we modern individuals view ourselves.

---

[5]New York: Scribners and Sons, 1929. pp. 177-78.

Every college freshman knows at least the rudiments of Freud's structural concepts of id, ego and superego, and in coffee shops you may overhear people talking of "complexes" and repression, even if they are not using the terms exactly.

Freud's model of the self proposed that beneath the level of our "polite" social selves, there lay a dark and dangerous region of socially unacceptable desires which were held in tenuous check by the superego and ego but which threatened to explode suddenly or leak out in strange and perverted ways. Perhaps this view of the "hidden" self was amenable to a Europe and North America whose view of man's soul had been colored by several hundred years of Calvinist-derived preaching about the human species' innate depravity, but in any case, Freud's id, as a sort of psychological base line, has become the way we modern people see ourselves, as creatures driven by dark, unwholesome desires that we don't fully comprehend, subject to a chaotic *eros* which is insatiable and potentially destructive if the fragile ego cannot mediate between the id's primitive urges and the superego's societal demands.

In his late essay *Civilization and its Discontents* (1930), Freud wrote of the dual nature of human beings:

> Starting from speculations on the beginning of life and from biological parallels, I drew the conclusion that, besides the instinct to preserve living substance and to join it into ever larger units, there must exist another, contrary instinct seeking to dissolve those units and to bring them back to their primeval, inorganic state. That is to say, as well as Eros, there was an instinct of death. The phenomena of life could be explained from the concurrent or mutually opposing action of these two instincts.[6]

Not only does the death instinct exist, Freud says, but human beings seem to revel in it. He writes, ". . . in the blindest fury of destructiveness, we cannot fail to recognize that the satisfaction of the instinct is accompanied by an extraordinarily high degree of narcissistic enjoyment, owing to its presenting the ego with a fulfillment of the latter's old wishes for omnipotence." This inclination to ag-

---

[6]James Strachey, trans. and ed. New York: W.W. Norton, 1961. pp. 65-6.

gression, says Freud, is "an original, self-subsisting instinctual disposition in man."[7]

For evidence, he had only to look at the carnage of the First World War and the upsurge of hatred that was beginning to stir among the Aryan nations.

By the turn of the century, then, the optimistic worldview of those who saw a sort of salvation in modernism was being undermined in several ways. Descended from the beasts, humankind was a seething mass of unlawful and destructive desires, but at least, we may suppose, they could take refuge in the fact that humans knew where they stood in the grand scheme of things, they had in their heads a cosmic map or picture that had been described in exquisitely accurate detail by the equations of Newton's *Principia Mathematica* (1687). At least God was in heaven and all was right with the cosmic order.

Alas, even that part of our collective world picture was collapsing. At work in Switzerland, Einstein was quietly rewriting the map of the Newtonian universe. In 1905, with the publication of his Special Theory of Relativity and then again in 1916 with the publication of the General Theory, Einstein shifted Earth's place from somewhere near the center of things to the outer edge of a not very significant galaxy swirling somewhere out in the suburbs of the universe surrounded by light years of emptiness. It was a world in which neither time nor space had objective reality, a world without straight lines.

Though Einstein through his life maintained that people should not draw philosophical conclusions from his science, it was inevitable that people did. He himself, in his non-scientific writings, waxed philosophic. Though in his work he kept insisting that God did not play dice with the universe, his search for some sort of Unified Field Theory which would tie together all the anomalies in his theories remains unsuccessful to this day.

The cat of relativity, however, had been let out of the bag, and it was inevitable that the "relativity" of the physical universe gradually became the model for relativity in ethics, values and spirituality. As has been true since Ptolemy, and probably before, astronomy and

---

[8]Ibid., pp. 68-9.

physics became the archetype of moral life in the modern world. And so, we in the twentieth century found ourselves tossed into a brave new world without map, rudder or compass.

Things were looking bleak indeed. Only a few hundred years separated the modern world and worldview from that of the Renaissance, yet what a chasm there seemed set between them. Imagine a modern reader, say the Hemingway of *A Farewell to Arms*, coming upon this passage from the *Oration on the Dignity of Man* by Pico della Mirandola (1463-1494) in which God addresses the paragon of his creation, humankind:

> We have set thee at the world's center that thou mayest from thence more easily observe whatever is in the world. We have made thee neither of heaven nor of earth, neither mortal or immortal, so that with freedom of choice and with honor, as though the maker and moulder thyself, thou mayest fashion thyself in whatever shape thou shalt prefer.[8]

In the modern world, as it was unfolding itself in the first half of this century, there was no center, no one choice that made sense over any other, no heaven, no God, no freedom, no honor. It was, as W. H. Auden dubbed it, an *"Age of Anxiety"* in which the individual seemed utterly abandoned in a world that had suddenly lost its intellectual and moral moorings. It was a world in which ". . . the historical process breaks down and armies organize with their embossed debates the ensuing void which they can never consecrate, when necessity is associated with horror and freedom with boredom . . . ."[9] For an individual in this unconsecratable world "there was no one-to-one correspondance between his social and economic position and his private mental life."

There seemed to be no vocabulary for the new modern reality. Certainly the old words did not apply to the brave new world and yet, as Pound wrote in *Hugh Selwyn Mauberly*, "The age demanded an image/Of its accelerated grimace."[10]

---

[8]Giovanni Pico della Mirandola. *Oration on the Dignity of Man*. Trans. A. Robert Caponigri. Chicago: Henry Regnery. 1956. pp. 7-8.

[9]W.H. Auden. *The Age of Anxiety: A Baroque Eclogue*. New York: Random House, 1946, p. 3.

Yet what image could be found amidst the shards of the world between the wars? And if the problem of finding an adequate world picture was difficult between the wars, what were we, as a species, to make of the ensuing developments that led through fascism and a second, more-embracing World War? What could be said of a war which saw some 52 million dead and wounded, half of them civilian, in which six million Jews and six million others were systematically and efficiently exterminated with modern technology, a war which ended with the unleashing of two atomic bombs which killed hundreds of thousands in two apocalyptic explosions? In many ways, this war seemed to confirm all the worst suspicions of the poets and writers between the wars and even made their pessimism seem inadequate.

In the 50 years since the end of the Second World War, the modern world has had blow after blow delivered to its self-esteem and sense of place—overpopulation and its attendant problems of hunger and war, industrial pollution on such a vast scale that the very climate of the earth has been changed, deforestation, desertification, holes in the ozone layer, all of this played out beneath the umbrella of the world's nuclear strategy of Mutual Assured Destruction.

And so the great anthropologist and historian of religion Mircea Eliade wrote in 1967:

> . . . the modern world is in the situation of a man swallowed by a monster, struggling in the darkness of his belly, or of one lost in the wilderness or wandering in a labyrinth which itself is a symbol of the infernal . . . and so he is in anguish, thinks he is already dead or on the point of dying, and can see no way out except into darkness, Death or Nothingness."[11]

This dark worldview has been labelled "modernism." It is an umbrella term which includes such diverse phenomena, people and movements as Picasso and Cubism, Surrealism, minimalism, LeCorbusier and the International Style in architecture; James Joyce, T. S. Eliot, Samuel Beckett; existentialists like Sartre and Camus; and the

---

[10]In John J. Espey, *Ezra Pound's Mauberly*. London: Faber and Faber, 1955, p. 119.

[11]Mircea Eliade, *Myths, Dreams and Mysteries: the Encounter Between Contemporary Faiths and Archaic Realities*. New York: Harper Torchbooks, 1967.

nearly endless list of writers, thinkers, artists and philosophers who have reacted to the conditions of the modern world with loathing, despair, black humor, or who have not despaired but have nonetheless hankered after something *more* than the switched-on modern world had to offer. Lurking behind modernism is an assumption that previous ages did not face a world as bleak and humanly unpromising as the one we inhabit. Some, like Beckett, saw that old world as an illusion, waiting for a God(ot) who was not likely to appear. Others, like Eliot and Yeats, seemed to feel a nostalgia and sense of loss for a world and worldview now shattered beyond recovery.

This distinctly modern worldview undoubtedly rose up out of the complex of social, technological, and intellectual changes that took place in such a rush since about 1880 and which led to the feeling that life in the modern world is more fast-paced, fragmented, centerless and alienating than it has ever been before.

Thus, "modernism" became a constellation or particular configuration of thought patterns which is recognizable immediately. It consists of dimensions that are simultaneously social, technological, intellectual, and even, to use an "unmodern" word, spiritual. The various elements of the complex are difficult to separate out, but when they are, we see that they form a recognizable pattern which fits our definition.

One may take virtually any aspect of what we call "modern" life—television, fax machine, computer, telephone, the visual arts, existentialism, deconstructionism—and see in it virtually the same pattern for all these modern phenomena—individually and collectively—have made our lives seem faster and more fragmented, and have separated us from individuals in ways that would be unthought of just 150 years ago.

The breakup is easiest to see on the level of day-to-day living, but it is happening in the world of ideas as well. Within universities there has been a sort of "ghetto-ization" of academic departments, so much so that it is now commonplace to say that academicians cannot talk to each other across disciplines anymore. The emphasis on specialization, abetted by the computer and the "information explosion," has led us off into fragmented worlds where we are alienated from others who do not share the language or argot of our narrow field.

The result is the current raging debate on college campuses and in local school systems about what ought to constitute a "curriculum."

The fast-pace, fragmentation, loss of center and alienation which characterize modern life can best be seen in the primary medium by which we in the modern world understand ourselves—television, a one-way medium whose hallmark is the speed with which it delivers to us the "news," i.e. the various bits of discrete and uncontextualized information that we have come to rely on to keep us informed about what is happening "out there."

As time has passed, we modern folk have even become accustomed to this fragmented state of affairs and could not imagine any other way of living. Luckily, most of us, afforded the option of nearly endless entertainment in the form of television, can dispense with even thinking too much about the lack of coherence in our modern world and the horrors that we have witnessed in the twentieth century. Perhaps we have finally found a way to "get used to it."

And, indeed, until we stop to think about it, we can perhaps fool ourselves into thinking that everything is all right this way, that there is something in all this that makes sense, that this modern life without a moral or geographic center is not so bad after all, especially since TV and advertising paint for us an extremely seductive picture of "the good life" which resembles so much the life we already live.

But times come—times of death, disease, natural destruction, war and violence—when we are confronted with ultimate and pressing moral and spiritual questions which will not be denied or avoided, and it is only then that we realize, perhaps, how centerless our modern lives really are, how few connections we actually have to things of lasting importance, how little "meaning" there is beneath the surface flash of the plugged-in world in which we live. There is, at the center, a void, as Sartre so clearly expressed it for his generation in *Being and Nothingness* in the late 1940's. Existence is severely limited, the natural state of human existence is anguish and anxiety. We human beings, and everything else which exists, are *de trop*, simply "too much" in a universe that is, at bottom, absurd. For Sartre and others, the only possible response to this, in a world devoid of God or gods, is a radical human freedom which creates *its own* existence continually—a heroic existential stance, but one which, after 50 years, has proved exhausting to the point of despair.

The Postmodern Dilemma

We catapulted our time traveller from 150 years ago into a world where not only the daily lifestyle was radically different, but even the basic operating assumptions, the underlying paradigms* by which we understand the world and our place in it, were virtually unrecognizable to him.

If it seemed to him that we moderns live a life without a center, it seems no less so to us when we actually stop and try to think about it at all.

The mental map, or picture of the world we carry around in our heads is composed of confetti, bits and pieces swirling around, names, images, pictures and sounds which refuse to organize themselves around a coherent center. In the final analysis, a revolution in Kurdistan, a rock star's new hairdo, a riot in Los Angeles, a new philosophical theory, all level out and become a piece of the whirling confusion of modern life that so disoriented our time traveller earlier in this chapter.

We in the late part of the twentieth century are living lives without centers. Our cities have no geographic centers anymore and our mental lives have gone off center, too. If there are any continuities at all in our time, they are that virtually every aspect of what we call "modern" life is experienced in a way that is fragmented, fast-paced and alienating.

In fact, it may not even be fair to call this way of life "modern" anymore. There is a new term for it, one that says that even the well articulated "modern" worldview is now *passé.* In retrospect, the "modern" worldview of modern art, of Yeats, Eliot and the others, at least had a nostalgia for a center that once existed, but the new worldview, if you can call it such, says that fragmentation, fast-pace and alienation are about all we can expect, and, in the final analysis, are about all there is.

That worldview, one without a map and without a center, a world in which compass bearings would be meaningless even if we could get them, is what I think is meant by the much-used, but rarely defined term "postmodern."

Most academics and art critics would agree that what was once defined as "modernism" in art, architecture, even philosophy has been supplanted by something "postmodern" in recent years, though hardly anyone will venture to say exactly what the new "postmodern" world-view actually is. As social critic Todd Gitlin notes, "Both art critics and academics agree something postmodern has happened, but no one knows exactly what it is."[12]

But Gitlin and others have attempted to isolate certain characteristics that seem to define an attitude that, for lack of a better word, has been called postmodern. If, as Gitlin notes, the characteristics of "modernism" in art, architecture and thought were anxiety, fragmentation and re-combination of elements (as in Cubism), and at least an aspiration to some sort of lost unity that was presumed to have existed in an earlier age (see writers quoted above), then "postmodernism" is a place where the search for unity and deeper significance has been given up. The center has been lost and the search for it has apparently been abandoned.

As Gitlin notes, it is a world where nothing seems to exist beneath the surfaces, where everything is about "textuality" and "intertextuality,"* where no meaning is fixed and all is relative.

"Postmodernism reflects the fact that a new moral structure has not yet been built and our culture has not yet found a language for articulating the new understandings we are trying, haltingly, to live with."[13] This understanding, in much of the art, popular culture and intellectualism of the period is characterized, Gitlin says, by "a collapse of feeling, a blankness, a knowingness that corrodes any positive principle."[14]

The postmodern world's prime expressive medium, whether consciously "postmodern" or not, is television, a medium which both creates and reflects a world whose very syntax is the random juxtapo-

---

[12] Todd Gitlin, "Post-Modernism: the Stenography of Surfaces." *New Perspectives Quarterly,* Spring 1989. p. 56.

[13] Ibid., p. 57.

[14] Ibid., p. 57.

sition of images. In a typical 15-minute segment of television, say a newscast, one may see a story on a tornado in Indiana followed by highlights of a Detroit Tigers game, followed by a story on famine in Ethiopia immediately next to a commercial for gourmet cat food. If one practices "channel surfing," as many viewers do today, then the fragmentation and dislocation is even worse. After only a few hours of this mindless surrealism, one ceases to notice anymore that "reality" can be experienced in any other way than rather arbitrary juxtapositions of pictures, sounds, and ideas all of which, in the end, blend into one another.

In the end, the postmodern worldview collapses in on itself and the main stance is ironic. It becomes a state of mind in which the fast pace, alienation and fragmentation of modernism are no longer upsetting, as they were to writers like Auden, Pound and Hemingway, but are rather seen as normal, even inevitable. To be hip is not to care. Indeed, "caring" in this jumbled context seems rather quaint, old-fashioned, in a word, "modern," and we're beyond that now.

Writing of postmodernism in art and architecture, critic Charles Jencks says, "The figure of man and woman that emerges is sometimes frail, occasionally mutilated and often paradoxical—an acknowledgement that our place within the universe, or even a technological civilization, is no longer as central as it was in the Renaissance."[15]   For Jencks, the fragmentation of postmodernism is " . . . a reweaving of the recent past and western culture, an attempt to rework its humanist tenets in the light of a world civilization and autonomous, plural cultures."[16]

Regardless of their conscious intentions, however, the postmodern architecture of Robert Venturi and Michael Graves, David Byrne's talking heads of mid-American banalities, the host of contemporary postmodern painters, critics and philosophers who draw their inspiration from everything from classical sculpture to Saturday morning cartoons reflect a world where incoherence, loss of center, and the relativity of virtually everything have been seen as the norm rather than as an aberration.

---

[15]Charles Jencks. *Post-Modernism: the New Classicism in Art and Architecture*. New York: Rizzoli International Publications, 1987. p. 11.

[16]Ibid., p. 13.

In his seminal postmodern document, *The Postmodern Condition: A Report on Knowledge*,[17] Jean-Francois Lyotard defined the dilemma. Though Lyotard's prose style can be sometimes mind-numbing, his basic point seems to be this: the traditional way of knowing who and where you were was through Narrative (e.g. mythology, religion). This Narrative mode of knowing was supplanted in the "modern" (post-1650 A.D.) world by Science* which claimed to be a way to objective verifiable truth. In our own times, however, the work of writers like Karl Popper and Thomas Kuhn and others has shown that Science itself is not reliable as a way to truth for science's "truth" can be valid only within a more or less arbitrary paradigm which gives it some "truth" relative to other "truths" within the paradigm but not any absolute "truth." (The very fact that the word truth must now be put in quotation marks indicates how far the basis for knowledge has been undermined in our time.) Thus, we cannot only not find our way to truth, there is simply no truth to be had. Everything is a matter of competing paradigms, interacting texts, and nowhere is an absolute connection to be found to anything that could be called universally true. (We will explore the evolution of this dilemma in more detail in chapters Three and Four below.)

The result, says Lyotard, is that "each individual is referred to himself. And each of us knows that our *self* does not amount to much."[18] If, as Lyotard indicates, we have lost confidence in the ability of our minds to identify anything as remotely "real," then everything is as true as everything else. Or as false.

In the academic world, those charged with pursuing the old abstract virtues of "veritas" or "scientia" are in disarray, having lost any common language to talk about issues outside their field. If they cannot speak to one another within the academic community, how much worse does it become when they try to speak to society at large, to the worlds of politics or economics, for example?

Lyotard writes:

---

[17]Geoff Bennington and Brian Massumi, tr., Minneapolis: University of Minnesota Press, 1984.

[18]Ibid., p. 15.

We may form a pessimistic impression of this splintering [of language and universes of discourse among and between academics, society, politicians, scientists, etc.]: nobody speaks all of those languages, they have no universal metalanguage, the project of the system-subject is a failure, the goal of emancipation has nothing to do with science, we are all stuck in the positivism of this or that discipline of learning, the learned scholars have all turned to scientists, the diminished tasks of research have become compartmentalized and no one can master them all."[19]

This, essentially, is the condition of twentieth century "modernism." As we've noted, however, what differentiates postmodernism from modernism is that the postmodern ceases to yearn for any other state. The postmodern individual has ceased to care that there ever was a center. As Lyotard says, "the mourning process has been completed. . . . That is what the postmodern world is all about. Most people have lost the nostalgia for the lost narrative."[20]

What is left? Lyotard presents us with a picture of the world that our time-traveller visited earlier in this chapter:

Eclecticism is the degree zero of contemporary general culture: one listens to reggae, watches a western, eats McDonald's food for lunch and local cuisine for dinner, wears Paris perfume in Tokyo and "retro" clothes in Hong Kong; knowledge is a matter for TV games . . . Artists, gallery owners, critics and public wallow together in the "anything goes," and the epoch is one of slackening.[21]

Echoing him, Tzvetan Todorov, writing in *The New Republic*, says, ". . .the salient feature of postmodernism is thought to be incoherence. . . ." Its characteristics are "the relativity of values, the dispersal and decentering of the subject, the limits of reason, the fragmentation of the world, the breakdown of dogmatic virtues and encyclopedic narratives."[22]

---

[19]Ibid., p. 41.

[20]Ibid., p. 41.

[21]Ibid., p. 76.

[22]Tzvetan Todorov. "Postmodernist Culture: an Introduction to Theories of the Contemporary" by Steven Connor. *The New Republic*. May 21, 1990. p. 32.

Clearly, this postmodern moment is not a happy period in intellectual history, and the late twentieth century is not a happy time in which to live. And yet, to paraphrase Wordsworth, it is in this postmodern confetti world that we must find our salvation or not at all.

In the end, perhaps, postmodernism is like the phenomenon it attempts to describe, both everywhere and nowhere at once. It defies definition. Postmodernism is nevertheless a useful term for our purposes if we allow it to denote a sort of late twentieth century *zeitgeist** that senses that we are ankle-deep in the pieces of a past that has inexplicably crumbled and that we have come to accept this state of affairs as normal. For better or worse, it is where we are as a culture, but it is also where we must begin. For, as Lao-Tzu pointed out over two thousand years ago, "The journey of a thousand miles begins with the ground beneath your feet."

And so we set out like early cartographers, blank charts in hand, compasses and quadrants at the ready, to map a world that, for all its familiarity seems, upon examination, to be utterly strange.

CHAPTER 2

The Topography of the City of God

AS YOU APPROACH THE CATHEDRAL OF CHARTRES, EVEN TODAY from the train station, you climb in a gradual ascent until you finally reach the top of the commanding hill on which the great building stands. Even to those of us jaded by the sights of a modern city sky-line, the first vision of the facade is awe-inspiring. Starkly outlined against the sky, the two unmatched spires draw the eye irresistibly upwards, reminding us, if of nothing else, that in a previous time the world of material objects was not a be-all and end-all but pointed be-yond itself to another world, another dimension to which this world was only the prelude and dim mirror image.

If the sight is impressive even to us, imagine what it must have been to those contemporaries who came on pilgrimage up the steep medieval way when the cathedral was new. There, carved in stone, was the history of the world to be read like a great book. In the cen-tral bay of the North porch, the pilgrim would find the beginning of human history with Adam and Eve and the fall that propelled them from the Garden. Opposite it, at the southern door, appeared the Church triumphant, with Mary as intercessor for the human race on judgment day. Here the pilgrim would see the end of the sacred his-tory that the story of Adam and Eve began: the souls of the saved going upwards into the New Jerusalem while the souls of the damned were forced downward into everlasting torment. In between, around the building, he would read the stories of the prophets, patriarchs and apostles carved in stone. Above the western door, illuminated by the last rays of the setting sun, he would see Christ the King sitting in triumph in a glorious depiction of the final Day of Judgment. The entire building tells the symmetrical and orderly story of salvation history* in which the second Adam redeemed the sin of the first by dying on the tree of the cross.

Inside this magnificent carapace the pilgrim would see the tremendous vaulted nave—again drawing the eyes heavenward—and at its easternmost end, closest to the rising sun, at the very "climax" of the architectural space, stood the altar whereon was re-enacted the sacred mystery of the Mass which, for a few moments, would draw together heaven and earth, past, present and future, the human and the divine and align them along a vertical axis of meaning, a union into which any believer in good grace could enter via the holy communion.

The skylines of the medieval cathedral cities are dominated by the vaulting naves and towering spires of the great churches which in former times formed the centers of the cities' social, economic and spiritual life. And they were apt centers indeed.

In their perfect Platonic* proportions, they were imitations of the original creation of the universe. As the centers of civic and spiritual life, they placed their communities right in the stream of sacred history, and, as images of the New Jerusalem to come, they pointed forward to the end of history when, in the Christian *mythos*,* all would be swept away into eternity, the horizontal axis of time would be abolished and the vertical dimension alone would remain. This was the significance of those great stone books set in the center of medieval life.

Otto von Simpson, in a study of medieval cathedrals, writes, "If the architect designed his sanctuary according to the laws of harmonious proportion, he did not only imitate the order of the visible world, but conveyed an intimation, inasmuch as that is possible to man, of the perfection of the world to come."[1]

Walking around an old cathedral town, even the modern-day tourist captures something of the atmosphere in which our medieval ancestors lived their lives. The great churches are located at the hub of the street plan, visible from every crossway. The old walls of the town form circles, the centers of which are these great piles of stone

---

[1] Otto von Simpson, *The Gothic Cathedral*. Princeton: Princeton Univ. Press, Bollingen Series XLVIII, 1988. p. 37.

standing there to remind us of the connection between this world and the next. The centrality of the mythic vision is inescapable.

In the great cathedral towns of medieval Europe, we can see clear evidence that spiritual ideas have tremendous power to shape the material world in their image. We in the modern world tend to discount the power of the spirit, attributing movements in history to shifting economic patterns, but in the world's sacred architecture we can see example after example where great material and economic resources were marshalled in the name of a transcendent,* non-material reality.

The point is this: the architecture of sacred buildings everywhere mirrors the harmony and proportions of a divine universe. These holy places refer to something beyond themselves. In former times, manmade architecture was modelled on the architecture of the Master Builder, God Himself. The world's architectural evidence reveals a world where the modern split between the sacred and the profane, between material and spiritual causes scarcely existed. One world informs the other and gives it its meaning. Von Simpson writes, "In this view, the perfect proportions, the beauty of which we may admire in musical and architectural compositions, also acquire an explicit technical or techtonic function: they chain and knit together the different elements of which the cosmos* is composed."[2] When a believer looks at a cathedral, walks into it, worships in it, he or she experiences the universe in its entirety. In that sacred place, all things become as one. Past and present, time and eternity, individual and God—these everyday distinctions become less important.

It is not just in European cathedrals, of course, that one experiences this arrangment of the profane world around a sacred center.

Orientalist Heinrich Zimmer in his *Artistic Form and Yoga in the Sacred Images of India*[3] shows how spiritual insights found three-dimensional form in the Buddhist holy temple city of Borobudur in central Java. This vast monument with its various plateaus and stupas* forms a four-sided world mountain made by humans in imitation of a divine model. Movement through the temple and up towards the

---

[2]Ibid., pp. 29-30.

[3]Princeton Univ. Press, 1984.

highest central plateau is meant to assist the pilgrim or worshipper to achieve his or her spiritual center. The crossing of many thresholds, passing through galleries crammed with sacred images, and climbing upwards through the several levels of this great monument are all intended to transform, gradually, one's state of consciousness. Leaving behind the horizontal realm of time, one journeys through the labyrinth* to the center and there finds coherence, unity and peace.

Standing atop a pyramid in the Yucatan or atop a ziggurat* in ancient Mesopotamia, one can look down and see the world of human habitation, the city, radiating outward from the sacred center, a perfect model of the order felt in the cosmos.

Whether it is an ancient cathedral city like Chartres or Reims, or a simple native American village with a lodge pole in the middle, we find throughout history that humans have traditionally constructed their lives around a sacred center.

From the modern or postmodern secular materialist perspective, the locations of these "centers" may seem arbitrary and, in a sense, they are—at least to non-believers. But when a Muslim bows towards Mecca several times a day, or when an American Indian travels by canoe to a sacred island, or a Christian or Jew enters a sanctuary, he is approaching a center that is as much inner as outer. This was clearly understood by our medieval ancestors. On the flagstones of the Chartres cathedral there is a circle-shaped labyrinth—some 300 meters long if stretched out in a straight line—to the center of which pilgrims would navigate on their knees as a sign of their having taken a sacred inner journey to the center of their cosmos.

When an individual or a culture organizes itself around such a common center, a focus and identity are gained which they would not otherwise have. With a clear center, the chaos of experience becomes the cosmos of meaning, the long meandering pilgrimage through the labyrinth of life has a destination.

With the cathedral at the center of their city and Jerusalem at the center of their world, medieval Christians could feel composed and confident in a way that we modern people find difficult to sustain. With a hearth fire, a lodge pole, a sacred mountain, temple or cathedral as a constant visible reminder of the fundamentally spiritual nature of the cosmos, the sacred mind could always find its bearings. The interpenetrating geography of the spiritual world and the material world is as complete and coherent as the order of a beehive where the millions of hexagonal cells are clearly organized around the queen bee. This is the topography* of the City of God: a human community arranged around a sacred center.

This was, in fact, the character of the first human cities ever built, in ancient Sumeria. Theologian John S. Dunne, in *The City of the Gods*, writes:

> The first cities, being temple communities, were places where mortals were thought to consort with immortals, where human kings consorted with the divine mother, sharing not only the experience of life but also the experience of death, and where the generality of mankind, often by participating vicariously in the experience of a king, acquired the knowledge of life and death which was thought to belong to the gods.[4]

It was a world of order whose focus was the point at which the vertical axis of meaning met the horizontal axis of time, where the commercial and social life of the village met the timeless, impersonal realm of the gods. And it was at that point that our ancestors established their center so that they could be aligned and in balance, existing in both realms at one and the same time.

We human beings seem to exist in two apparently contradictory environments at the same time. While one part of us proceeds along the timebound path of aging and death, the other part of us exists in a place which feels timeless and eternal. While one part of our brain is occupied with the future and "progress," another part longs for the deep past and stasis. Up and down the spinal cord go the conflicting messages of our existence: pay the rent, get the promotion, find the ultimate meaning of life, eat, defecate, praise God, fear the Devil, drive the BMW, immerse yourself in the oneness of all things, move on, stay still, grow, change, procreate, die.

Language, much less logic, fails utterly to keep up with the ceaseless flow of it all.

---

[4]John S. Dunne, *The City of the Gods: A Study in Myth and Morality.* New York: Macmillan, 1965. p 218.

And so, in the midst of the confusion, we plant a stick in the ground, or draw a magic circle, or build a temple, or somehow create a holy space with a clear center and organization where, if only briefly, all the mutually contradictory realities of our human existence may be reconciled. We need to "disappear" occasionally into this ritual* time and space—whether it is by meditating on a prayer mat in a spare room or attending Mass in a thirteenth-century cathedral. We need, on a regular basis, to find a place inside and outside ourselves where oppositions are banished and contradictions are reconciled, a place where there is no longer an "I" or "they," no "me" separate from a God, no "we" separate from nature and the cosmos, a place where all is unified.

From the postmodern perspective, of course, bowing to Mecca, praying a rosary or chanting the monotonous monosyllabic Buddhist sutras achieves nothing. From the outside, such repetitive actions look like neurosis, perhaps symptoms of a compulsion disorder. The view from *within* the ritual process, however, is quite different, for the practitioner *experiences* a change in his/her normal relations to self, other people and the cosmos at large.

The organization of the City of God, as we've defined it here, helped the individual to do this. In a society which possessed a sacred geography, the individual had no trouble locating himself or herself for there was always a center. This is the reason, despite physical geography, that medieval cartographers always placed Jerusalem at the exact center of their maps and why, along the margins, far from the holy center, they put dragons and monsters. For this reason, the cathedral stands at the center of the medieval city, the ziggurat stands at the center of the ancient Babylonian city and the pyramid formed the civic and spiritual center of Mayan civilization. The physical geography of the world and the organization of the city of Man had to correspond to the spiritual geography of the unseen universe, otherwise nothing made sense.

Dunne again:

The first cities, those built in the Tigris-Euphrates valley, were essentially temple communities and were conceived to be the home of the gods, and each of the more important cities of the Nile valley was thought to be the site where creation had taken place and where the gods had come into being. There was probably in the building of the cities in Mesopotamia with their ziggurats . . . some feeling of throwing up a tower that should reach to the sky. . . . The principal temple at Erech, for instance, was called Eanna, the House of Heaven, the dwelling-place of An the god of the sky and Innin, his daughter, the goddess of the city, and its walls were spoken of with pride as touching the clouds. To live in Erech was to consort with An and Innin, to become as one of the gods.[5]

Now let us look at the city of modern and postmodern man and contrast it with the holy cities of days gone by. We will find it an unholy place at best and, at its worst, absolutely infernal, for in the modern city, the divine connection is lost. Dunne writes of the evolution of the city, "What has happened, it seems, is that the hope of consorting with the gods has been given up and been replaced with the simple hope of consorting with human beings."[6] It is a hope that, in our times, seems increasingly hard to fulfill.

The Modern City of Man

Approaching the modern city, one sees cathedral spires, if at all, tucked away, barely able to peek above freeway overpasses. Dominating the skyline in the way that old cathedrals used to are those hybristically-named inventions of modern architecture, skyscrapers, built mostly by banks, insurance companies and corporations. In older modern cities, these impressive spires are clustered together in a commercial center or downtown where the central banking district is or was.

Architecturally, we have seen this sort of organization before. The modern skyscraper is, in one sense anyway, the functional geographic equivalent of the cathedral. It forms a center of the city's social, spiritual and economic life. Scraping the sky, these commercial needles may even give the impression of performing the unifying function of a world center,* but there is one crucial and overwhelmingly important difference. The skyscraper, unlike the cathedral, does

---

[5]Dunne, p. 30.

[6]Ibid., p. 33.

not speak to anything beyond itself. In spite of its verticality, it speaks only of and to the horizontal axis of money, time and economy. There is no cause greater than itself to which the modern skyscraper is dedicated.

As if there were any further need to demonstrate that mammon had rather definitively displaced God in the modern age, some early skyscrapers, like the Woolworth building in New York, were even modelled after medieval cathedrals, complete with gargoyles, spires and buttresses. In the final analysis, the modern city organization, unlike those of human communities of the past, became, in Harvey Cox's famous phrase, the secular city.

If we look at what could be called the "postmodern" city of Man, the situation is even worse, from a spiritual point of view, for the old "modern" city at least had some sort of center, even if its purposes were merely financial. The postmodern city, dubbed by journalist Joel Garreau the "Edge City," does not even have the semblance of a center, not even a merely economic one. This is the city of the modern North American (and increasingly worldwide) suburb which is laid out on a line and which consists mostly of commercial strips lined with muffler shops, fast food restaurants and shopping malls.

It is an unholy place, both aesthetically and in the sense we have been speaking of. An aerial view of an ancient holy city will show, generally, a clear center with the rest of the community organized around it and culminating, often, in a wall, as in the medieval towns with their church or cathedral at the center and their walls, with gates opening to the four major directions, forming the circumference. An aerial view of the post-modern "edge city" will show something that looks like a boa constrictor which has swallowed several rabbits. A thin line of asphalt or concrete, four or five lanes wide, forms the body of the snake and periodically you will see bulges of commercial developments, mostly near large freeway interchanges.

Life in and around these edge cities is strictly linear and is made possible by the internal combustion engine. Like the medieval cathedral town, the edge city is a perfect likeness of the worldview of the people who live, work and shop there. The organization of the strip city is a mirror in which we see a society which has no clear view of a coherent and meaningful spiritual universe. Rather, the edge city is as fragmented, alienating and fast-paced as the world which created it. Traffic along the primary commercial strip is quick, hostile and broken up by frequent stops, "turbulence" in the parlance of traffic engineers. It is strictly commercial with no space at all for spiritual uses which might take up valuable commercial real estate. If money is the god of the late twentieth century, then the mall is its cathedral and shopping its primary ritual. You think of other, higher realms along these strips only at peril of your life, for if you are trying to find a world center in such a place, you may be quite quickly sent heavenward by someone making an illegal turn into the nearest fast food restaurant.

It is a scene we are all too familiar with in the postmodern world. In the midst of plenty, there is spiritual poverty. Poet and scholar Kathleen Raine articulates the problem eloquently:

> The typical city of the materialist civilization may meet a certain 'standard of living' in matters of housing, amenities, water-supply, sanitation and the rest, employment, social services, all those things which were the object of Utopian Communism or 'the American way of life' with its superabundance of material goods. What is notably lacking in cities built without the vision of the 'heavenly original' is any trace of beauty, where the eyes can rest and find peace or delight. There may be stupendous works in terms of size, productivity, efficiency, but the soul is starved. We never feel at home in the absence of beauty, we wander the streets . . . but we never find home.[7]

This is the life into which our nineteenth-century time traveller was suddenly propelled back in Chapter One, life without a center, life lived along the horizontal axis at 60 miles per hour, a life generally agreed by its more thoughtful residents to be without much connection, grace or meaning.

Is it fair, really, to compare the modern commercial strip with ancient Babylonian ziggurats or medieval cathedral towns or are we

---

[7]Kathleen Raine, *Golgonooza, City of Imagination: Last Studies in William Blake.* Hudson, NY: Lindisfarne Press, 1991. p. 118.

merely setting up an easy target to illustrate how far downwards we have come in our rapid fall into the postmodern world?

The answers are, respectively, yes and no. Of course it is fair to compare the modern commercial strip, with all its fast food franchises and muffler shops, to a medieval city for where a civilization puts its economic and emotional resources is a reflection of its spiritual values. In that sense, what you see, architecturally, is what you get spiritually. In the middle ages people spent vast amounts of time and money to pilgrimage to shrines or the Holy Land. Today the object of the travel is more likely to be the mall or Disney World. In a spiritual society, people hope to see the face of God. In a postmodern one, they opt for Mickey Mouse.

As for the second question, isn't the commercial strip, and the lifestyle it represents, too easy a target, I believe the answer is no. We have, one way or another, come to accept this disjointed state of affairs as normal. We have not yet realized the full implications of what we've created. We have come to believe, as a culture, that this life without a spiritual or moral center is not only inevitable but may even be *good* for us.

One could perhaps use the analogy to pollution. Growing up as a child along Lake Erie, I took it for granted that cities would dump raw sewage into waterways, that lakes were industrial dumps, that having "No Swimming" signs posted everywhere was the price we paid for progress. At some point, someone had to point out that it was not the natural state of lakes to be dead.

The same was true of the use of pesticides which, by the mid-century, were simply taken as inevitabilities, even boons to the human race. It took Rachel Carson with her *Silent Spring* and a handful of other early environmentalists to point out what ought to have been obvious—that we were killing significant parts of the natural world and, in the process, were killing a part of ourselves.

Today, spiritually, the situation is analogous. Somehow, without noticing, with the best of intentions even, we have polluted the spiritual environment of the human species. In the name of progress, we have attempted to do what no other culture in our human history has attempted: to live life without a spiritual and a moral center. By most accounts, this experiment has failed.

The evidence of its failure should be as obvious to us as was the evidence of pollution forty years ago. Conservative analysts like Allen Bloom and E. D. Hirsch have been first to recognize it. In America, Ronald Reagan and George Bush built political campaigns on it. But liberals, too, with their political emphasis on issues like the environment and economic justice, are clearly aware of the problem.

There is no question that in America, over the past fifty years, there has been a widespread erosion of traditional beliefs and morals, followed by a decay in traditional family organization, an incredible rise in the use and abuse of addictive drugs and mood/mind-altering substances, a horrific rise in violent crime especially among the young, social decay, environmental waste, political corruption, degradation of the global environment, warming of the atmosphere and a general sense that unless things change for the better we are living at the end of times, in an age of lead. These are all symptoms of life without a center. Large numbers of us are lost in the middle of nowhere without compass, map or guide.

Yeats feared it in 1919. "The center cannot hold," he wrote.

Today, many feel we lost the center long ago and sometimes we may ask ourselves, "How would we even recognize a center if we found one?" One way is to continue to study the topography of the old cities of God and to link that sacred geography, whenever possible, to the innermost needs of the human heart.

What the Center Does

Imagine yourself standing alone on a great plain somewhere. From your vantage point there are six primary directions—four horizontal ones (front, back, left, right) which correspond with your face, back, dominant and inferior sides. Then there are two vertical directions—"up" to a region which is accessible only to birds and those strong enough to climb mountains and "down," a place which is accessible, at least to a point, to anyone with a shovel. To the horizontal dimension belong the things of this world: procuring food, shelter, finding companionship. To the vertical dimension belong the things of the gods: the weather, the sun, life in the form of plants coming up from the ground, death in the form of things being subsumed back into the earth.

The center of all this, the center of the world, in effect, runs right up the spinal cord of each individual. It is from the center of the self that each of us measures front, back, up, down, left, right. The self should carry its center with it wherever it goes and so a feeling of dislocation should never occur, but, of course, it's not that simple. The self is always in flux, ever changing, always moving. It may even be experienced as "chaotic." The flow of time carries this everchanging self along like a boat on a river and we have trouble maintaining a hold on it.

The whole business is complicated by the fact that no one is born alone. Each human being is born into a community of some sort, each member of which presumably experiences himself or herself as the center of the world. What happens when groups of individuals—each a world center—attempt to live together? One would expect to see a sort of social chaos everywhere one looks, but this is not the case. Anthropologists note that virtually every human culture has figured out some method of providing a sense of order, center and community for itself, usually through shared myths and rituals. Almost universally, communities seem to establish, via their myths and rituals, agreed upon world centers where the "I" is subsumed into the "we." In the sacred space, the distinctions between self, community and the realm of the gods are banished and a common center is established. It is this world of shared belief, or shared center, that is so lacking in the postmodern world we've been discussing.

In our normal everyday consciousness, we experience the relationship among the self, others and the cosmos as separate, something like this:

This is the postmodern worldview where we experience nothing but fragmentation, separation, non-connection. From this point of view, one gets the impression that the self is somehow disconnected from the community and the cosmos. One's individual ego seems to loom large and alone. This is the view of our "secular materialist" culture where the self is put in first position with the needs of others and the earth itself coming in a distant second. In its more self-aggrandizing moments, the individual inflates beyond all bounds and may feel him/herself to be far more significant than is really the case. Conversely, in negative moods, the self in this situation may feel cut off, alienated from others, fragmented, alone, in a word "modern."

As will be developed below, the function of ritual in human societies is to dissolve the separation between self, others and the cosmos and give the self an experience of unity, coherence and wholeness. During the ritual process, the feeling of fragmentation disappears and we experience the three elements of self, community and cosmos in quite a different relationship. For when we enter into the ritual time and space, we experience things as unified, as pictured in the following relation:

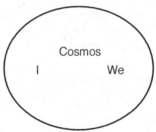

The point at the which the three circles of self, others and the cosmos overlap is the realm that we call the sacred and it is simultaneously located both inside and outside the self. The purpose of creating special sacred places, or of constructing the sacred city, is to provide us an outer place in which, for the fleeting moment of the ritual, we may experience the true and underlying reality of our existence which is that all the separations which we experience in our everyday life are, in reality, merely manifestations of some underlying unity, whether we call it God or Brahman or mana or power or Being. The fragmentation and alienation we experience are all illusory, not manifestations of the way things *really* are.

The need for a center, whether it is a lodge pole in a plains Indian tent or a stupa in India or a cathedral in a medieval town, seems to be one of the primordial needs of the species. It is nothing less than the need for coherence and order.

The world center—sometimes imaged as the world tree or world navel—is the meeting point of the sacred and the profane, which is another way of saying it is a meeting point for the contradictory parts of our very own nature, for we are beings in whom the worldly preoccupations and the sacred aspirations co-exist uneasily most of the time. At the world center the horizontal plane of everyday time blends with the vertical plane of meaning.

Often this world center is imaged as a sacred mountain (Olympus for the Greeks, Mt. Zinnalo for Laotian Buddhists). Human imitations of these sacred mountains take the form of ziggurats, pyramids, altars, etc.—places where the sacred and the profane intermingle. Mt. Calvary in Jerusalem formed one such center for the medieval mind and the altar raised within the cathedral was a visual echo of that sacred mountain on which, in the Mass, the union of the divine and human, of body and spirit, of community and individual and Godhead which took place on the original Calvary was repeated on a regular basis.

The world center could also take the form of a tree which, with its roots in the earth, its trunk in the middle and its branches reaching up to the sky, also serves to connect the lower, middle and upper realms. Yggdrasil for the Teutons and the cross of Christ for the Christians were two such "world trees," the cross of Christ having double power by its placement atop the "world mountain" of Calvary.

Almost the only vestige we moderns have of this symbolism of the center is the annual ritual of the Christmas tree, which has its roots in Teutonic mythology, and perhaps if we explore the symbolism of that common sign it will be easier to see what we have lost in the postmodern world. The Christmas tree creates within the home a small world axis. Bringing the tree indoors abolishes the usual distinction between outside and inside. The fact that it is "ever green" shows that life continues in the midst of winter's death. Most families buy a tree that stretches from floor to ceiling like the world tree extending from earth to sky. Topping the tree off with a star or a glass spire of some kind reminds us of the tree's original cosmic nature as the world tree uniting the heavens, the earth and the underearth. The tree is strung with lights so that it brings light to the darkest time of year. We then hang animal and human-shaped ornaments (bears, nutcrackers, toy soldiers, etc.) on the tree branches to remind us nostalgically of Yggdrassil, the world tree on the branches of which we mortals dwell. Beneath this amazing tree, as befits a world center, we find on Christmas morning a profusion of gifts, the bounty of a harmonious cosmos, which have magically appeared during the night.

Here we have a vestige of the feeling of what life must be like continuously for people whose lives are organized around a sacred world center, and it is the very antithesis of the geography of nowhere in which most of us today normally live. Life in the postmodern world, as we will explore below, is merely a pale echo of the geography of somewhere in which the Western world used to dwell.

CHAPTER 3

The Geography of Somewhere

IN CONTRAST TO THE POSTMODERN WORLD'S "GEOGRAPHY OF nowhere," people in previous ages seem to have had a better sense of where they were located, in a cosmic sense at least, than we do today. In this country, surprisingly large numbers of people are looking into ancient and "foreign" religions in an attempt to find the missing center. In this search, one hears the terms "western" and "Eurocentric" used quite often in a pejorative sense as though that tradition were so spiritually bankrupt that there is no sense in turning to it anymore. Indeed, the searches for meaning that many of us in the west have undertaken are motivated by the widespread feeling that the religions of our tradition have nothing to say to the world we live in.

It might be worthwhile, however, to look back in this western tradition to a time not that long ago when the sacred* and profane were still connected in our minds. The point of doing this is not to "rescue" Western Civilization which lately seems to have been rather cavalierly tossed aside by many intellectuals, but merely to show that what we call "Western" thought has not always been inimical to the world of spirit. There is nothing wrong with looking to other historical traditions in our search for the center. In fact, researches into Oriental practices, Native American mythologies and other esoteric traditions are an indispensible part of the contemporary western world's task. But the center whose loss we are currently suffering was *our* center, no one else's, and it therefore might be instructive at this point to return to the last moment in western history when religion seemed to function fully in its role as a mythological worldview*.

In the late sixteenth and seventeenth centuries, we find a time and place in Western history where belief in an ordered earthly and heavenly cosmos still reigned. God was still in *his* (not her) heaven, and, standards of political correctness aside for a moment, human beings knew where they stood in relation to him. This period in European history marks a sort of intellectual watershed between the older, more coherent world of the Middle Ages and the brave new postmodern world in which we find ourselves today. It was a world on the verge of modern science, but one in which people could still summon up an all-embracing metaphor—the Great Chain of Being*—which revealed the bounty of God's creation, its order and its ultimate unity.

Barely one hundred years after Columbus' first voyage, only 50 years after Copernicus' *De Revolutionibus* (1543), it was still largely a world of corresponding planes in which the angelic, the human, the divine, the social and the bestial mirrored each other and served as metaphors for each other. It was a world picture* of an ordered universe, a place where every detail belonged to a coherent whole.

In this world of correspondences, we find a view of humankind quite different from the modern view. Everything, including that microcosm* of the great universe, the human being, had its divinely ordained place in the order of things. In this belief, poised between the angels and the beasts, we find a human animal with a spark of divinity within. In this world, humans contain in themselves all the elements and all the faculties of the universe, from the godlike abilities of reason to the animal passions of the body.

To hearken back to Pico della Mirandola's *Oration*, quoted in the first chapter, human beings possessed the finest qualities of all the animals and, by grace of the free will given to them by their creator, could fashion the earth in any form they saw fit.

Imagine a world without chaos—or, if you will, a world in which what we call "chaos" is believed to be part of the dark inscrutable workmanship of God, a world in which there are no accidents, no acausal events, no fragments, a world where everything "fit."

The metaphors used back then suggest what such a world would feel like. The harmonious interconnections of the world were imaged as music, dance and crystal spheres nesting inside one another. Everywhere one looked, one could observe the divine order. The whole was reflected in every part and all was orderly.

In Thomas Elyot's *The Boke Named the Govenour*, we find this worldview articulated quite clearly:

> Hath not God set degrees and estates in all his glorious works? First in his heavenly ministers, whom he hath constituted in divers degrees called hierarchies. Behold the four elements, whereof the body of man is compact, how they be set in their places called spheres, higher or lower, according to the sovereignty of their natures. Behold also the order that God hath put generally in all his creatures, beginning at the most inferior or base and ascending upwards. He made not only herbs to garnish the earth but also trees of a more eminent stature than herbs. Semblably in birds, beasts and fishes some be good for the sustenance of man, some bear things profitable to sundry uses, others be apt to occupation and labor. . . . Every kind of tree, herbs, birds, beasts and fishes have a peculiar disposition appropered unto them by God their creator. So that in everything is order, and without order may be nothing stable or permanent. And it may not be called order except it do contain in it degrees, high and base, according to the merit or estimation of the thing that is ordered.[1]

This is the order that so informs the worldview of Shakespeare's plays. In *Troilus and Cressida*, Ulysses delivers a sort of poetic sermon on this order:

> The heavens themselves, the planets and this centre
> Observe degree, priority, and place
> Insisture, course, proportion, season, form,
> Office and custom, in all line of order;
> And therefore is the glorious planet Sol
> In noble eminence enthron'd and spher'd
> Amidst the other, whose medicinable eye
> Corrects the ill aspects of planets evil
> And posts like the commandment of a king,
> Sans check, to good and bad. (I, iii, 85-94)

---

[1] Thomas Elyot, *The Book Named the Governor* in *The Renaissance in England*. Eds. Hyder E. Rollins and Herschel Baker. Lexington MA: D.C. Heath. 1954. p. 107. For a full explanation of this worldview, see E.M.W. Tillyard, *The Elizabethan World Picture*. New York: Vintage Books, n.d.

When everything functioned as it was intended to within this divine order, the world and the human beings within it participated in a grand cosmic dance, here imaged by Milton, in his *Comus* (1637), as a Morris dance, an English country dance of exuberance and fertility:

> We that are of purer fire
> Imitate the starry Quire
> Who in their nightly watchful Sphears
> Lead in swift round the Months and Years—
> The Sounds, and Seas with all their finny drove
> Now to the Moon in wavering Morrice move.[2]

The driving force of all this cosmic harmony and motion was God's love, as Sir John Davies wrote in his *Orchestra* (1598):

> What makes the vine about the elm to dance
> With turnings, windings and embracements round?
> What makes the loadstone to the north advance
> His subtile point, as if from thence he found
> His chief attractive virtue to redound?
> Kind nature first doth cause all things to love;
> Love makes them dance and in just order move.[3]

Examples like these could be multiplied endlessly, but it should be clear enough by now that these people believed in an ordered universe in which human beings had a rightful place. There was, of course, disorder from time to time in this neat, hierarchically* ordered universe. In fact, continuing his speech above, Ulysses in *Troilus* indicates how disorder manifests itself.

> But when the planets
> In evil mixture to disorder wander,
> What plagues and what portents, what mutiny,
> What raging of the sea, shaking of the earth,
> Commotion in the winds, frights, changes, horrors,
> Divert, crack, rend and deracinate

---

[2] John Milton. *Complete Poems and Major Prose.* Ed. Martin Y. Hughes. Indianapolis: Odyssey Press. 1957. p. 92.

[3] Quoted in E.M.W. Tillyard. *The Elizabethan World Picture.* New York: Vintage Books. n.d. pp. 104-5.

> The unity and married calm of states
> Quite from their fixture. (I, iii, 94-101)

To see how deeply the Elizabethans feared the disruption of the cosmic order, one need only read Shakespeare's great tragedies, virtually every one of which involves some break in the Chain of Being and the inevitable tragic consequences. Disruption of the order causes ghosts to walk in *Hamlet*, children to forget their fathers in *Lear*, madness throughout the plays, storms and earthquakes. In *Macbeth* horses turn cannibal and day becomes night. Indeed, it is the very picture of the chaotic, fragmented postmodern world that Ulysses paints, continuing in *Troilus and Cressida*, for if "degree" or hierarchical order is taken away, the result is the sort of world we see around us:

> . . . Each thing meets
> In mere oppugnancy. . . .
> Strength should be lord of imbecility,
> And the rude son should strike his father dead;
> Force should be right; or rather, right and wrong,
> Between whose endless jar justice resides,
> Should lose their names, and so should justice too.
> Then everything includes itself in power,
> Power into will, will into appetite;
> And appetite, an universal wolf,
> So doubly seconded with will and power,
> Must make perforce an universal prey
> And last eat up himself. (I, iii, 109-124)

It reads like a summary and analysis of the front page of any metro daily newspaper in the world.

What makes these old tragedies different from the modern ones, however, is that in the end, the divine order always reasserts itself, even if it means grinding up a few protagonists along the way. There is the sense, as Hamlet says, that

> There's a divinity that shapes our ends,
> Rough hew them how we will (V, ii, 10-11)

In fact there *is* a special providence in the fall of a sparrow, for everything is divinely ordered.

In a way that may seem initially surprising to us, this world-view of Shakespeare and his contemporaries has more in common with primal or tribal worldviews than with the modern worldview with which we now live.

Like the Elizabethan, the members of primal groups believe in a world without accident, a world neatly organized around a world center, which lends coherence not only to the physical landscape but also to the mental landscape of those who organize their lives around it.

Unlike the modern person who lives life primarily along the horizontal axis of time, both the Elizabethan and the Australian aborigine organize their lives around the vertical axis of meaning and see order where we see chaos, find significance where we find random coincidence.

This vision is neatly summarized in this famous illustration [See Figure 1] of the macrocosm* with its concentric spheres organized around the orb of the Earth and the corresponding diagram of Elizabeth whose own body magically encompasses the concentric spheres of society and the qualities of majesty. Here, the *primum mobile** of the large universe is paralleled with the queen as the first mover of the social and political spheres. One could produce yet a third diagram of an individual human being, also consisting of a hierarchy of powers and faculties which perfectly mirror the harmonious organization of both the universal macrocosm and the larger body politic.

Schematic diagrams of this sort, of course, are ideals. Even in Shakespeare's time the cracks were beginning to show. One need only read the history plays to see how largely loomed the fear of immanent disorder. The causes of this, of course, were largely political and partly biological. (It was becoming clear that Elizabeth was going to die without an heir and this obviously caused a great deal of anxiety.) But in addition to political and economic sources of unease, there was also a new movement in the intellectual world as well, a sort of shifting of the intellectual spheres, for this period of history, from the early to the late seventeenth century, also saw in Europe the beginnings of what was to become the dominant mode of thought of the modern world, science.

The most important invention of science, of course, was science itself, that is, the scientific mode of thought. This new way of thinking—which demands analysis, physical proof, repeatable and controlled experiments—proved to be such a powerful intellectual tool that, over the past three hundred years in the west and increasingly through the rest of the world, it has virtually driven out other modes of thought or relegated them to the scrap yard of mythology and superstition.

The invention of this new way of thought did not come full-blown, of course. The seeds of it were planted early in the history of the western world and flourished, often side-by-side, with the more synthetic, allusive, metaphorical way of thought that led to meaning rather than information. As early as 600 B.C., the Pythagoreans, to name only one group, were beginning to look at the phenomenal world as a place capable of being described by numbers. That movement died out, but the impulse to describe the phenomenal world remained and manifested itself in Aristotle and the thinkers who traced their lineage to him over the next two thousand years.

But it was only in the mid-to-late seventeenth century in Europe that science claimed its place as the pre-eminent mode of thought. It was as though at this time, the years between about 1650 and the late 1700's, the western intellectual world tried on a new set of lenses and discovered, to its amazement, that parts of the world which previously appeared fuzzy or out of focus suddenly came into brilliant relief.

We moderns look upon the time as an age of intellectual heroism, the Enlightenment, the Age of Reason, and, therefore, it is somewhat shocking to turn to the early scientists like Harvey, Boyle, Halley, even Newton, and find them talking in terms that we today would find totally "unscientific."

The earliest modern scientists saw themselves as interpreters not of a purely *natural* world, but of a world that was merely a mirror of a supernatural order that existed both above and within the world of appearances. From our perspective, they made surprisingly little distinction between the horizontal realm of time and the vertical realm of meaning, but seemed to have believed, in what may seem to us a decidedly *medieval* way, that study of one would reveal the other.

In a very detailed and well-written study of this period, Richard S. Westfall has traced the relationship between science and religion in

Figure 1.

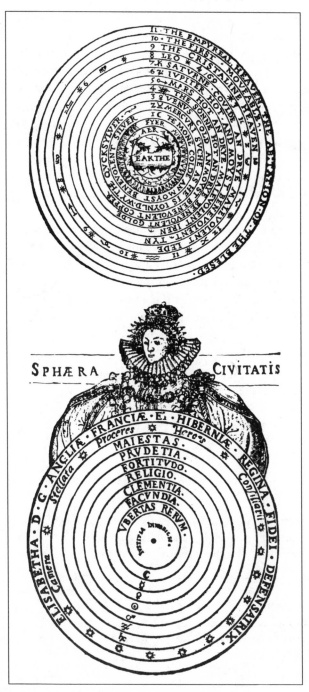

the scientific work of the first modern scientists, known collectively as the *virtuosi*.*

In the writings of these early scientists one can discern a genuine attempt to keep intact the older "sacred" worldview, or, in our terms, to describe the physical world in terms which would not contradict the order of the spiritual world in which they firmly believed.

As Westfall writes, "For the *virtuosi* the study of nature and the perception of her beauty were positive religious experiences. To them the world was not a meaningless turning of gears and wheels; it was an order instinct with the intelligence of the Creator, a mighty testimony of His grandeur, worthy to display His glory. Nature's declaration of the Creator's glory inspired them with a feeling of awed surprise which runs as a theme throughout their works."[4]

In work after work, these early scientists attempt to move scientific knowledge forward without abandoning their sacred experience. Astronomer Edmund Halley even composed a poem to serve as a sort of preface to the first edition of Isaac Newton's *Principia Mathematica* (1687) which illustrates that the motivation of the early scientists to explore and reveal the order of the universe was largely religious:

> Behold the regions of the heavens surveyed,
> And this fair system in the balance weighed!
> Behold the law, which (when in ruin hurled
> God out of chaos called the beauteous world)
> Th'Almighty fixed, when all things good He saw!
> Behold the chaste, inviolable law![5]

Or this expostulation on his motives, written, in prose, by the chemist Robert Hooke (1635-1703):

> 'Tis the contemplation of the wonderful order, law, and power of that we call nature that does most magnify the beauty and excellency of the divine providence, which has so disposed, ordered,

[4]Richard S. Westfall, *Science and Religion in Seventeenth Century England*. Ann Arbor: Ann Arbor Paperbacks, 1972, p. 27.

[5]In *Sir Isaac Newton's Mathematical Principles of Natural Philosophy and His System of the World*. Trans. Leon J. Richardson, Ed. Florian Cajori. New York: Greenwood Press. 1988. p. xiii.

adapted and empowered each part so to operate as to produce the wonderful effects which we see; I say wonderful because every natural production may be truly said to be a wonder or miracle if duly considered.[6]

These early scientists seemed to have believed firmly in a universe of meaning which was waiting to reveal itself through this new way of looking at it. Fundamental to this worldview was a belief in the continuity of things, that the realm of the spirit was reflected in, even embodied in the physical world, that, under it all, there were no accidents for the universe was the product of a rational God who ordered things in a way discoverable by his creatures. There is, throughout the writings of these early scientists, a sense of awe in the face of a God-created universe and a firm belief that beneath the apparent randomness of the surface phenomena there would be found a universal and meaningful order. Robert Boyle, the chemist, wrote:

> For the works of God are not like the tricks of jugglers, or the pageants that entertain princes, where concealment is requisite to wonder; but the knowledge of the works of God proportions our admiration of them, they participating and disclosing so much of the unexhausted perfections of their Author, that the further we contemplate them, the more footsteps and impressions we discover of the perfections of their Creator; and our utmost can but give us a just veneration of His omniscience.[7]

One cannot imagine such stuff being printed in scientific papers today, except, perhaps, those that come out of Bible colleges.

Eventually, however, God and science had to part ways. The attempt to reconcile the ways of God to man was gradually abandoned—at least by science—as it became increasingly clear over the next couple of hundred years that one could not reach spiritual harmony by pursuing an increasingly fascinating course along the horizontal axis of time and history and knowledge. Gradually, like the widening of a split in a log as the narrow edge of the wedge drives itself in, the rift between the spiritual and the scientific modes of

---

[6] In Westfall, p. 31.

[7] In Westfall, p. 42.

thought grew wider until, in the "modern" era, the chasm between the two has seemed to most to be unbridgeable.

By the late nineteenth century, as we'll try to trace in the next chapter, the sacred and the secular* worlds had become quite separated as the scientific mode of thought mounted triumph after triumph in its ability to describe the physicial world. It was a view determinedly horizontal, historical and material for what scientists eventually realized was that in order to do science, they had to believe that the physical world was a world composed only of matter, a world in which non-material (i.e. spiritual) forces did and do not operate. (If you think is not true, then try to tell a scientist that something happened "miraculously" and see how far you get.) The scientist must also assume that this material world is capable of being accurately known and described by human intelligence alone.

This is the unique underpinning of the scientific worldview that evolved in Europe in the mid-to-late seventeenth century. So impressive was this new method of thought, that even the dry wit of Alexander Pope was driven to rhapsodize on the author of the *Principia Mathematica*:

> Nature and Nature's laws lay hid in Night:
> God said, *Let Newton be!* and all was light.

Well, not quite *all*, we might say today, for between that time and ours what had once seemed light now sometimes seems like the brightness in a fog, where there is no shortage of light but where, nonetheless, things are not clearly seen at all.

The ongoing debate in America between so-called Creationist science and mainstream science over the question of evolution only illustrates the confusion that the rift between the worldview of science, which has become the mental "world" in which most of us live, and the world owned by "religion" has caused.

What science has convinced us of, intentionally or not, is that, given enough time, the method of thought evolved by the seventeenth century *virtuosi* and perfected in laboratories and universities over the past three and a half centuries will yield answers to all of life's most pressing and urgent problems. It has convinced us that objective knowledge is worth more than subjective experience, that mathematics (including statistics) yields more valid results than poetry, and that science is the royal road to Truth, with a capital T, while virtually all else is "mythology," a word which, tragically, has come to be synonymous in general usage with "falsehood."

There is no point in making science the bogeyman of this chapter. That's certainly not my intention here. No one living in the latter part of the twentieth century can deny that the strides made in medicine, public health, communications, and general living comfort have been immense and welcome. But these advances have come at a cost and the cost has been a virtual bankruptcy of the spirit which has become one of the dominant themes of modern art, literature and music.

In fact, of course, the problem is not "science" itself, but rather something that the ancient Greeks, the first inventors of the scientific way of thought, seemed obsessed with in their great tragedies. It is the problem of *hybris*,* an overweening pride in our own cleverness that, as Sophocles illustrated so well in his *Oedipus Tyrannus*, can lead us to the giddy and ultimately destructive belief that we control our own fate. This fault is what generates and brings to catastrophe the story of Oedipus.

Post-Freud, we have difficulty remembering that the initial fault of the drama is not that Oedipus killed his father and married and impregnated his mother. In Sophocles those are merely the *outcomes* of the prior sin of Laius, Oedipus' father, who attempts to outwit fate as prophesied at Delphi and sends his infant son off to die on the mountainside and instead triggers the series of events which leads to plague, destruction, death, incest, blindness and catastrophe well into the next generation.

The *hybris* that virtually all we moderns are guilty of is essentially the same as that of Laius and Oedipus. We, too, have come to believe that we may, at no peril, ignore the messages of the spiritual world, that we may, without risk, pay no heed to the vertical dimensions of our existence. We have convinced ourselves, blindly, that all of our problems may be solved here on the horizontal plane, by application of the proper scientific technique.

The result has been, as we have seen, a sort of "soul death" in the modern world. It has brought us to the place of no place, the world of fragmentation and alienation that we call modern and postmodern life.

Like a tragic hero poised on the edge, our own overweening pride has brought us to the brink of catastrophe. The language of our time is the language of crisis on nearly every front. The situation is desperate. As usual.

In the great tragedies, *hybris* leads, inevitably, to destruction. The catastrophe is mitigated, somewhat, by the protagonist's insight, an insight we the audience are allowed to share without paying the terrible price of our lives.

If, indeed, we in the postmodern age are at a turning point in our collective history, is it possible for us to gain the insight we need without suffering catastrophe first? In other words, is it possible to find our way back to the center where meaning and experience are united?

That is the vital question we need to keep in mind as we consider what life would be like in a world where more attention was paid to the vertical dimension of meaning than we seem willing to give it.

CHAPTER 4

The Journey to Nowhere

THE JOURNEY TO NOWHERE—TO THE PLACELESSNESS AND DIS-
jointedness of postmodern life—was not a deliberate one. That is,
those early searchers into the scientific way of thought did not intentionally set out to bring us to confusion. If anything, their intent was
just the opposite. Armed with what seemed to them an invincible
weapon in the war against ignorance, they set out to conquer human
fallibility, and to answer, finally, age old questions of creation and
the origin of life and death in such a way that we could at last be
certain about their validity. Ironically, however, the Western search
for direction, clarity and certitude that began so confidently in the
Age of Reason, led, 350 years later, to the indirection, confusion and
uncertainty of postmodern life.

It might be good here to provide a quick sketch of Western intellectual history over the past 350 years so that we can appreciate
both how swiftly the fragmentation came about and also see just how
recently the last vestiges of the traditional, holistic Western worldview fell away. The idea is to show that the intellectual trends of the
past 350 years are not irreversible but rather might represent a temporary false turn, an experiment which looked promising but which,
from the postmodern perspective, needs to be revised. In the several
thousand year history of the Western tradition, a false turn of three
and a half centuries may not really constitute a tragedy—not if, that
is, we are willing to reevaluate the assumptions under which we've
been operating since the Enlightenment.

"I think, therefore I am."

In the last chapter we saw that as recently as the late 1600s there still functioned a holistic worldview in which all the parts of the inner and outer universe operated in synchrony and sympathy. It was a world without accidents in which each part and each event played—or was presumed to play—a meaningful role. The sacred and the profane were still believed to be intimately related to one another. God was presumed to take an active part in sustaining the order of creation and human beings were seen as the linchpins of creation, occupying a status between the beasts and the angels. Humans possessed divine reason, an image of God's own intelligence, which would soon be able to solve the riddles of the universe and, if not see God, then at least understand him more fully through his creation.

Among the first, and certainly the most influential of the great Enlightenment thinkers to try to lay a certain foundation for human knowledge was Rene Descartes.

Descartes (1596-1650), the inventor of analytical geometry and calculus, put his faith in mathematics, for the laws of mathematics seemed to him to be universal, outside the reach of time and history. The theorems and formulae of mathematics were true in the ancient past and would continue to be true into the distant future, in fact into eternity, for unlike things in the physical world of extension, the ideal interrelationships of mathematics would never change. It was clear to Descartes that if we sought knowledge of the world that was certain, true and immutable, that knowledge would have to be expressed in terms of numbers.

But before he could begin to express the real world outside himself through the means of the ideal formulae of mathematics, he had to prove that there was a real connection between the objective outer world and the ideal inner world of his own subjective mind. To do this, he introduced his method of systematic doubt* in his famous *Discourse on Method* of 1637, the full title of which indicates its ambitious intent—*Discours de la Methode pour bien conduire sa raison et chercher la verité dans les sciences.*

Basically, the method was simple. Descartes systematically began to strip away all the knowledge he possessed that was handed down to him uncritically, which was based on faith or hearsay or on possible misapprehension. This included not only religious precepts but even such common sense realities as the existence of his own body, for anyone who reflects even for a moment will realize that the evidence of the senses is often unreliable. One can put a warm hand into a bucket of room temperature water and think it is cold while someone else puts a cold hand into the same water and thinks it warm. In the end, Descartes cannot even prove he is sitting in his chair in his study, for all of it could be a carefully constructed illusion. Was there, then, any one thing that he could be absolutely sure of? If there were, then he would have an incontrovertible starting point for rebuilding all the knowledge which he had so methodically stripped away. Knowledge, at last, would be based upon solid foundations rather than mere faith.

Of course, he found that starting point in his famous *"Cogito, ergo sum."* While he could deny and doubt everything else, there was one thing he could not deny—that he, Rene Descartes, sat there thinking. Therefore he, the thinker, must exist. Finally, he realized, knowledge could have a secure foundation, for at last there was one *fact.* His very doubting thoughts proved beyond a shadow of a doubt that there was something which could not be doubted and that was that he existed. And if *he* existed, then what else followed from that?

The world that Descartes reconstructed from his starting premise was, of course, the modern world as we understand it today. As Descartes laboriously began to build up again the edifice of knowledge, he created a worldview that we immediately recognize as our own in its major features. Ideas, especially those formulated in the language of mathematics and logic are universal, uniform and constant. The *cogito,** or thinker must exist, but the precise relationship between the thinker and his body cannot be determined. This becomes one of the main dilemmas of modern and postmodern thought—the divided self and how to bring it back together again.

This idea of a split or separation between the body and spirit is not new to Descartes, of course. It is as old as Plato's division of the ideal from the world of appearances, and was incoporated into Christianity in the notion of the soul existing in the body as a more or less separate entity which would depart, intact, at death to live forever while the body decayed. After Descartes, however, the distinction between mind and body sharpened in Western thought. Having introduced critical doubt or skepticism* into the philosophical dialogue, Descartes and his followers could never quite get things back together again, for how are we to know, really, if the thoughts the thinker thinks have any relation to the world "out there"? How can we even be sure our body exists? After all, a body may not be necessary for a disembodied thinker to think. When my mind seems to instruct my hand to pick up a pen and write, is it really the mind running the show or are the mind and body operating separately?

A sort of vertigo sets in as one asks these questions, and Descartes and his followers tried to deal with it in their own terms. Descartes' Dutch disciple Arnold Geulincx (1624-1669) proposed that the mind and body operated like two clocks, each keeping the same time. One clock chimes on the hour but the other one doesn't. If we look at the silent clock at the top of the hour and simultaneously hear the other clock chime, we might erroneously conclude that the first clock *caused* the second clock to ring, but of course we would be mistaken.

Similarly, the Cartesians say, mind and body follow parallel but independent courses. Both have their motions governed by the harmonious clockwork of God who wound up the mind and body and the intricate mechanism of the universe in such a way that when I think I am ordering my hand to write, in fact my hand is operating on its own. Mind and body are really acting independently of each other, both of their actions being like the independently turning gears of the clockwork universe.

This device of *occasionalism* rather uneasily bridged the gap between mind and body, spirit and matter, yet when all is said and done, it is clear from our postmodern perspective that the logical mind cannot really prove what every four-year-old already knows intuitively, that the mind and body, spirit and matter are already connected, not separate, that the mind does control such voluntary actions as movement of the arm, etc. Common sense does not even question it, but uncommon sense does—and thus Western thought crawled into a maze of forthrights and meanders created by logic that logic could not free it from. The crucial first steps had been taken, however, and once you put your faith in logic as the only valid method of inquiry and source of answers, then you must follow things through to their logical conclusions, no matter how "illogical" those conclusions may be.

The material world, for Descartes, consisted of extension and motion. These were innate ideas, independent of the senses, and as such were primary qualities. Our senses merely perceive such secondary qualities as taste, smell, texture, color, etc. The primary qualities of the physical world could be measured, quantified, translated into mathematical formulae and thus be understood. Physical particles, or "atoms," in motion made up all of reality. At bottom, all of these "atoms" are the same and must operate by the same laws. Like a piece of wax which may be molded into various shapes but still remain wax, so physical reality can assume many forms—rocks, plants, animals, the human body—and yet still be subject to the same underlying universal laws, laws which might be expressed in terms of mathematics.

As was suggested in Chapter Three, this insight was experienced by contemporary Europeans as a lifting of the veil. You have only to look at the sudden leap forward in the years between 1650 and 1700 to see the enormous liberating and energizing effect of this new assumption. From Boyle's Law in chemistry to the overtowering *Principia Mathematica* of Newton, these Cartesian assumptions had the effect of opening up the human mind and letting the sun of knowledge in. It is not for nothing that the period was called the Enlightenment, and the Western mind, armed with its new method, marched forward confidently. These things we know: the physical world consists of space or extension, motion causes all change, and mathematics is the best, if not only, way to express the interrelationships among these things.

This shift in thought set the West off on a remarkable journey of discovery and achievement unmatched and unparalled in human history. But there was a price to be paid for making the universe and human beings into machines and nothing but machines. By accepting the premise that everything is rigidly determined according to mechanistic principles, we set ourselves up for a sort of soul death, for soul and matters of the spirit seem to defy the mechanical laws of science. They refuse to cooperate. Fortunately for the scientists, souls and spirits did not have physical extension, were not, therefore, measurable, and could thus be ignored. And ignore them we did, right up to the present day.

The intention of the original scientists and philosophers of the Enlightenment was to bring all things together under the umbrella of reason, but the effect was to drive the world of spirit and the world of matter far apart. Through his method of "systematic doubt," Descartes reduced the self to merely the thinking *cogito,* in his famous formulation *"Cogito ergo sum."* Reason and logic were elevated over feeling and emotion. Knowledge replaced wisdom as the goal of learning. The measurable physical body took over attention from the unquantifiable soul, and changeable matter took on more importance than eternal spirit. The result has been that over the past three hundred years, as the Western intellectual community continued in the direction that Descartes had set out in, there has occurred, in the words of philosopher William Barrett, a sort of "death of the soul," as all those important elements of human experience which used to belong to the realm of soul or spirit became increasingly devalued. Modern academic psychology is merely walking in Descartes' shadow when it attempts to reduce all human emotion to the firing of neurons. There is, of course, no question that there is a biochemical component to what we call feeling, but one does not *experience* the release of the neurotransmitters, one experiences something much less atomistic, much more holistic, something that used to be named one's "soul." Alas, poor soul, you are unweighable, unquantifiable, intangible and, therefore, ignorable.

But the human soul could not simply be replaced by a vacuum. Somehow what had been "soul" or spirit had to be accounted for in the new mechanistic way. A new metaphor for spiritual development had to be developed, and it was the English philosopher John Locke (1632-1704) who provided it with his famous image of the mind as *tabula rasa.*

The Blank Slate

In his "Essay Concerning Human Understanding," begun in 1671, Locke attempted to determine the scope and limits of the human mind. His method was thoroughly rational and his conclusions were empirical. Following Descartes in the search for valid under-pinnings for human knowledge, Locke asked how we come to know things. Rejecting the notion of innate knowledge, Locke said that the human mind, at birth, is a *tabula rasa*, a blank slate. Like the ancient Roman *tabulae* on which letters were incised by pressing with a stylus, the mind was impressed by sense experiences, one after another, over the course of a lifetime. Beginning with these simple "ideas of sensation," the mind could then, upon reflection, assemble the simple impressions into more complex ideas. According to Locke, these two modes of thought, impression and reflection, are the only sources of knowledge. One must rule out divine inspiration or inborn ideas because God, being a spirit, cannot make sense impressions and the mind, being a blank slate at birth, can have no ideas prior to life experience.

In Locke's view, the mind was a mechanism that operated on mechanistic principles. If we today see this model as somewhat lacking, we should remember that to the followers of Locke, it was a great and liberating revelation. The implications of Locke's model for education and social reform were tremendous, for if each human infant comes into the world as a blank slate to be formed wholly by environment, then the potential for creating a perfect human society exists. All we need to do is provide the blank slates with beneficial (i.e. rational) experiences and these will impress themselves on the mind in such a way that social evils like violence, drunkenness, bestiality, etc. will simply disappear within a few generations. Over the next three hundred years after Locke, we have been trying, with only middling success, to educate people out of human frailty. Certain branches of psychology, e.g. behaviorism, are still searching for the exact mechanisms by which the perfect environment might shape the perfect individual.

Once again, as with Descartes, what was once called "soul" disappeared before the light of reason and intellect. The rational intellect became the arbiter of truth.

But what if the intellect itself were not trustworthy? Suppose that the conclusions it reached could be questioned? Then, having already dispensed with the world of spirit, what would we have to fall back on?

The Age of Reason, having neatly removed the realm of the spirit from the mainstream of intellectual thought and elevated reason into its place, needed only one more element to bring into full existence the thoroughly modern mind. That missing element was, of course, skepticism.

Descartes, in his famous *Discourse on Method,* used "systematic doubt" to remove all but the thinking mind, but systematic doubt was not the same thing as skepticism, for Descartes also invoked God at crucial moments in his discourse. After Descartes and Locke, however, the ultimate authority for truth became the rational human mind. And if the mind had become the ultimate authority on matters of truth, then it only remained to point out how feeble the mind was to make the modern worldview complete.

This was the job of the eighteenth century philosophers David Hume (1711-1776) and Immanuel Kant (1724-1804).

Doubting Everything

Scottish philosopher David Hume was the embodiment of the enlightened thinker. Beginning with Locke's *tabula rasa* theory of knowledge, Hume proved that there were limits to the abilities of human reason to know, with any certainty, anything outside such purely mental realms as pure mathematics. And even the rational world of pure mathematics was only as good as its premises were valid. Beyond that, he said, we human beings can only have probable knowledge.

Using unflawed logic, Hume then proceeded to show that even such a basic notion as causality could not be proved with any certainty. If one billiard ball strikes another and the second one moves, one cannot *prove* that the movement of the second ball was *caused* by the movement of the first. One may be dealing only with coincidental movement and a habit of mind. Harking back to the motion of Geulincx's two parallel but unrelated clocks, Hume proceeded to show that, in effect, nothing can be known or predicted with any certainty. Henceforth, skepticism would reign supreme as the intellectual's attitude towards not only the world of spirit but to the world of experience and ideas as well.

The German philosopher Immanuel Kant tried to answer Hume's skepticism with his *Critique of Pure Reason* (1781) by saying that in fact the mind can have knowledge *a priori* of things like causality because the intrinsic nature of the mind contains such categories as cause and effect for understanding the world of phenomena.* This was good, for it at least gave some certainty *within* the mind itself, but there knowledge ended for, following in the tradition of Plato, Descartes and Hume, Kant could not provide a rational connection between the world of perceivable phenomena and any other, more encompassing, non-physical world not accessible to the senses. According to Kant one can never know the *noumenal** world behind the phenomena. The really real is inaccessbile to the senses and therefore unknowable. And so, once again, the world that for centuries had been called the world of "spirit," the world that lies along the vertical plane of meaning, was regarded as inaccessible to the modern mind.

Science vs. Religion

Over the next two centuries, the schizoid rift between the vertical and the horizontal dimensions of our being only got wider. Mind-body, spirit-matter, sacred-profane were no longer seen as complementary realms but as opposites separated by a great gulf. Intelligent people of every stripe struggled to reconcile the two ways of thought, but the balance was clearly tipping in favor of the scientific mode of thought.

Less than 200 years after the first *virtuosi* confidently began to use their science to study God's order, we find God nearly invisible and certainly reduced in stature. From the mighty creative spirit who animated the entire phenomenal world, he devolved first to a mere watchmaker who, though he had created and wound up the mechanical universe *ab origine*, had long since retreated to allow the mechanism to fend for itself. This period of eighteenth-century deism was a sort of halfway station to postmodernism for it, along with the philosophical developments discussed above, definitively severed the string that linked the sacred and the profane and set mankind adrift in a mechanical universe which ran according to the impersonal laws of an unpersonified Nature.

The way of the future, to those living in the Age of Reason, belonged to science and intellect. To go the other way was to retreat into the darkness of medievalism. The best minds of the time moved forward into Enlightenment and the rest would have to catch up or live forever in night. The future, they confidently believed, would be freed from superstition. It would be a world of reason, light and science.

By 1800 or so, the division between the sacred way of viewing the earth and the profane way had widened and the split of the post-modern mind had begun. Among the educated and politically influential, the way of reason, empiricism and logic (i.e. materialism) held sway while the spiritual view of the earth and humankind became the property of those considered too feeble to comprehend the sophistication of this powerful new worldview—the poor, the ignorant, imbeciles, children, most women, and, of course, artists of virtually all stripes. Not surprisingly, it is during this period that we find a new idiom emerging from poets, artists and musicians who, reacting against the rational coldness of the Enlightenment, valiantly tried to apotheosize* Nature, emotion, passion and the irrational in spite of the major intellectual trends of the civilization in which they lived. This was the thrust of nineteenth-century Romanticism which, to judge by the marginalization of the arts in contemporary society, never really succeeded in overthrowing reason's monopoly on "truth."

In spite of the Romantics, more and more nineteenth-century thinkers and intellectuals—and even artists—turned to human reason rather than divine inspiration as the source of information about the world and cosmos. The scientific mode of thought continued to make stride after stride in its understanding of the world while, more and more, the role of the arts and the artists was to put on the brakes, to challenge the mainstream, to fly in its face even. Clearly the gap was widening. In the Renaissance, an artist like Michelangelo or Shakespeare could be the voice of the culture's main beliefs. In the modern world, this was less and less of a possibility as the mainstream values became inimical to the values of the spirit.

Then, in 1859, came the publication of Darwin's *The Origin of Species*, which exploded whatever tenuous dialogue was still left. It is not an exaggeration to say that *Origin* was perhaps the most important book published in the nineteenth century, more influential, in the long run, than even *Das Kapital*. One would be hard put to find any book to rival it in importance since Copernicus' *De Revolutionibus* (1543), for Darwin's book revolutionized the way we look at the biological world and our human species' collective past in the same way that Copernicus' work changed the way we look at the stars. *The Origin of Species* became—and still remains—a sort of intellectual barricade across which secular humanists and religionists throw fire bombs at one another. For the scientific mind, *Origin* provided a sort of secular Genesis, a rational, alternative *mythos* to the antiquated superstition of the Bible. It seemed to produce, at last, the sort of absolute knowledge of human existence that had been previously lacking. This was the sort of thing that had been promised by the builders of the scientific mind. To the religious mind, however, even today, the book amounts to an ontological* threat, for if *Origin* is "true," then how can the Bible not be false?

Not surprisingly, the reaction to the publication of *The Origin of Species* was more or less instantaneous. Religionists immediately saw the theological implications of what Darwin, through twenty years of exhaustive research and collation of data, had produced. And so the scientific worldview, developed so meticulously by Descartes, Locke, Hume and the rest, finally ran full speed into the religious worldview and we still have not finished sorting through the wreckage.

The shock wave did not result from the idea of evolution* itself, of course. That had been around for some time. In fact, Erasmus Darwin, Charles' grandfather, had been a proponent of some form of evolution in the late eighteenth century. What the early evolutionists did not understand was the mechanism by which species changed. This is the hole that Darwin's *Origin* filled with the notion of Natural Selection,* a process by which an impersonal "Nature," not a personal God, sorted out those most apt and fitting to continue the Struggle for Existence.

Thus, from the war of nature, from famine and death . . . the production of higher animals directly follows. There is grandeur in this
view of life, with its several powers, having been originally
breathed by the Creator into a few forms or into one; and that,
whilst this planet has gone cycling on according to the fixed law of
gravity, from so simple a beginning endless forms most beautiful
and most wonderful have been, and are being evolved.[1]

In this summation by Darwin, there is no more than an echo of
the religiosity of the earlier *virtuosi*, a mere token acknowledgement,
painting, as it does, a God who is even more remote than the God of
deism. Here God, if he is involved in the process at all, is perhaps
more like a potter than a watchmaker, idly tossing a lump of clay on
to a potting wheel and then allowing the clay to mold itself according
to the laws of momentum and chance.

Such a challenge could not go unanswered, of course, and so in
1860, there was a famous meeting of The British Association at Oxford University, the purpose of which was to debate publicly Darwin's theory and its theological implications. This now-famous debate, and its outcome, may be read as a sort of archetype of the battles that have followed. In it, we see that the modern, scientific
worldview was no longer the property of only a few intellectuals and
philosophers but by 1860 had gained an acceptance that soon was to
become a critical mass which would put an end, in respectable intellectual circles anyway, to the old medieval worldview which still believed in such non-physical phenomena as spirits, gods and miracles.

On the side of the angels, so to speak, was the Anglican Bishop
Samuel Wilberforce, also known as "Soapy Sam" for his bluff and
crowd-pleasing oratorical skills. His main life interests were in
church administration and the education of clergy. He does not seem
to have been particularly qualified to speak about science, though he
was an amateur naturalist and had reviewed *The Origin of Species* in
The Quarterly Review in 1860. His opponent, however, was well-
suited to the defense.

---

[1]Charles Darwin, *The Origin of Species: Volume II*. Chicago and New York: Rand,
McNally and Company, 1872. p. 186.

He was T. E. Huxley, at that time professor of Natural History at the Royal School of Mines. Darwin himself was ill, suffering, as later biographers have hypothesized, from a chronic tropical disease he had contracted while on his famous voyage aboard *H.M.S. Beagle*.

According to contemporary accounts, Wilberforce held forth that evening with his usual wit and bombast, winning over the crowd at Darwin's expense, while Huxley sat quietly in his chair. In a final mocking *coup de grace*, Wilberforce turned to Huxley and asked him whether it was through his grandmother or grandfather that he was descended from an ape.

The audience loved the joke, but Huxley saw it as an opening for a counterattack for as he had sat there, quietly, gravely, listening to Wilberforce, one thing had become clear to him. Wilberforce did not know what he was talking about—or, in kinder terms, the ancient religious paradigm out of which Wilberforce attacked Darwin was about to collapse beneath the weight of scientific evidence and thought.

Rising to the speaker's podium, Huxley announced that he was there only in the interests of science. He then went on, cooly and rationally, to explain that Darwin's theory was more than a simple hypothesis. Briefly and clearly, Huxley—whose gift as an orator was that he could bridge the gap between hard science and the common mind—demonstrated the bishop's ignorance of what Darwin had really said and put forth the proposition that Darwin's was the best explanation of how the various species evolved that had yet been advanced.

Then, in his own rhetorical *coup de grace*, Huxley turned to Wilberforce and said he would not be ashamed to have a monkey for an ancestor, but he would be "ashamed to be connected with a man who used his great gifts to obscure the truth."

As Huxley concluded, so the tale goes, men cheered and women swooned, so overwhelming was the victory of the scientific way of thought over the spiritual. As the century went on, Huxley became the champion of Darwin, publishing *Evidence as to Man's Place in Nature* (1863) and *Evolution and Ethics* (1893) and promoting through all his life and works the Victorian certitude that a thorough, rational understanding of the laws of nature and life was possible and that someday this scientific way of thought would lead to a perfected society which was scientifically and rationally controlled.

For a brief, optimistic period in the late nineteenth and early twentieth centuries, things looked good for science. With Newton's calculations to describe the physical world and Darwin's theory to describe the biological world, it seemed as though it was only a matter of filling in a few details before mankind's knowledge was complete.

One hundred and some years later, we know that the victory was less than total, for even towards the end of the 1800's anomalies were appearing in these apparently irrefutable theories, and in our time we have come to see that *all* theories are inaccurate and incomplete. From our postmodern perspective, there are no answers; there may not even be any meaningful questions.

We can use the ongoing debate between so-called Creationist science and mainstream science over the question of evolution to illustrate the rift between the world of science, which has become the mental "world" in which most of us live, and the world of "religion." It is a gap that is wider than ever, and the fractious debate going on in some circles today between Creationism* and Evolution illustrates the central problem confronting the modern and postmodern mind— what we may *believe* about the relationship between an individual, his society and the cosmos can no longer be reconciled with what we *know* about those things. In order to reconcile them, we must either compartmentalize our lives in a rather schizoid way—putting articles of faith in one box and articles of knowledge in another—or we must perform considerable mental gymnastics which try to collate emerging scientific data with Biblical accounts.

Valiant attempts are made to bring the two worlds back together, but they are not wholly satisfactory. One famous example of this sort of mental balance beam workout was the nineteenth-century fundamentalist idea that the fossil evidence put forth by the Evolutionists did not prove either that Darwin was correct about one species evolving into another or that the earth was enormously older than the Biblical account would indicate. Their answer as to why one could find sea shell fossils at the tops of mountains? God had created them on one of the days of creation and had simply sprinkled them around on mountaintops as a sort of *jeu d'esprit.*

Not surprisingly, nineteenth-century scientists and Victorian intellectuals lost their faith in droves. It was T. E. Huxley, in fact, who coined the word "agnostic"* to describe his own attitude regarding the world of the spirit. The neo-logism is significant for its root is *gnosis*, or knowledge, and without *gnosis* of God, agnostics proclaim, they cannot believe. Indeed, if one actually had knowledge of God, belief would not be necessary.

From the perspective of a hundred years, it is possible to stand back and see that both sides of this debate are simultaneously right and wrong. In effect there is no real debate here for debate about an issue can only take place if both participants are speaking the same language about the same problem. In the debate between the "religious" worldview and the "scientific," however, it is now clear that two separate languages were being spoken all along. Words, like "truth," that mean one thing along the horizontal plane of science might mean something quite different along the vertical plane, but since the word is used by both camps, confusion results.

Almost without realizing it, what had once been a unified language, as late as the seventeenth century, had devolved into an intellectual Babel in which we only apparently are speaking to each other. In 1680, one could speak, in the same breath, of God and Nature; by 1880, that was increasingly impossible.

Gnosis vs. Mythos

It might be worthwhile, at this point, to stand back, in a rather postmodern way, and try to sort out this Babel so that we can begin to understand what the debate has been about and to lay the groundwork for what is to come.

First, let's look at the religionists in this debate. It was perfectly natural for them to confuse religion with science for, up until fairly recent times, they were the same thing. To find out about the universe was to find out about the God of the Bible. To reject Evolution because it did not accord with Genesis was to ask the Bible to be a book of fact not a book of faith. Until the evolution of the "modern," i.e. scientific, mind it was not necessary to make a distinction between fact and faith because what we "knew" about the world coincided so closely with what we believed that the two could be reconciled. But as new knowledge began to outstrip the ability of faith to incorporate it—and this occurs, probably, in the second half of the nineteenth century—then bitter debate was unavoidable. That debate inevitably became more fractious and even silly for, quite without realizing it, both sides were shouting at each other in two different languages, arguing on two different planes, without being aware of it.

If the religionists made the mistake of elevating their spiritual book to the level of science, however, the scientific mind often elevates its way of thought from mere *gnosis* to *mythos*, taking secular knowledge for spiritual wisdom. If the underlying premises of the scientific way of thought outlined above in Chapter Three are correct, then science and the scientific mode of thought have no business commenting on matters that lie along the vertical plane of meaning, and yet this has inevitably happened.

In all fairness, it should be said that most reputable scientists resist making metaphysical claims for their work. Darwin himself chose not to comment on the theological implications of his theory and, in our century, Einstein said of his relativity physics that people should not draw moral or theological conclusions from his scientific ideas. And yet even he could not resist, in his writing, attempting to connect the two:

> If one conceives of religion and science according to these definitions, then a conflict between them appears impossible. For science can only ascertain what *is*, but not what *should be*, and outside of its domain value judgments of all kinds remain necessary. Religion, on the other hand, deals only with evaluations of human thought and action: it cannot justifiably speak of facts and relationships between facts.[2]

This sort of division between knowledge and morality seems a bit disenguous on the part of scientists and not wholly satisfying for the human mind cannot long stand discontinuity and irreconcilable oppositions, nor can it long endure compartmentalizing morality on the one hand and knowledge on the other. It will have unity—or pay the price.

---

[2] Albert Einstein, *Ideas and Opinions*. New York: Bonanza Books, 1964. p. 45.

And the price, as we have seen, is the schizoid nature of modern and postmodern life, its fragmentation, alienation and centerlessness. Religion is fragmented from science, faith from knowledge, logic from sentiment, self from community and all that lies along the vertical plane of meaning seems dissociated from the knowledge that lies along the horizontal plane of time.

In the late nineteenth and early twentieth centuries, there was tremendous optimism that eventually *gnosis* would lead to a sort of intellectual *parousia**, a new electrified Jerusalem where all the effects of what had been called "sin"—crime, disease, death, poverty, moral perversion—would be healed by the progress of science and the new social sciences. Thus, we would enter a brave new world that, as T. E. Huxley hoped, would be ruled by the law of reason.

Alas, no sooner had this hope been articulated than the scientific paradigm itself began to break down, and after a century of social and civil engineering, we seem no closer to Jerusalem than we were before. In some ways, when one looks at the hell of the modern urban ghetto and the global threats to life on the planet, we seem even further away.

And so we arrive at the fragmentation and alienation of the postmodern world. In many ways it has been a journey to nowhere, though the more hopeful among us are still looking, like modern physicists, for some sort of Grand Unification Theory which will pull together the modern knowledge we have of the world and unite it with the spiritual longing we have to fulfill the needs of our larger spirit.

This problem of reconciling the world of spirit and the world of matter is nothing new, of course. In fact, as we shall explore below, this disunity of the self may even be something endemic to human consciousness as it has evolved, and continues to evolve. The very words we use imply the nature of the problem. The word "religion," for example, comes from the same Latin root as the word "ligament," suggesting that some original experience of unity was lost and needs to be "re-ligamented," the bones rejoined. The idea of some sort of divided self is found in the East as well where the word "yoga" comes from the same Indo-European root as our English word "yoke" and, like religion, means to link together. The various *asanas** of *hatha yoga,* for example, are meant to link together mind, body and spirit. As described in the *Baghavad Gita,* all the various yogas—of knowledge, of discipline, of duty—have as their object a reunification of a split-off self with Atman/Brahman, the ground of all Being. And so, perhaps, the divided self is an ontological phenomenon.

What is unique about our time, however, is that this split which has been there, perhaps, since the first evolutions of a distinctly human consciousness, has grown so wide as to feel unbridgeable. Worse may be that in our *hybris* many of us seem to believe that it is not even necessary to heal the breach. Continuing in the empirical tradition, we believe that meaning will eventually arise from facts, but it should be clear by now that the vertical will never arise out of the horizontal way of thought.

What is called for in our time, I feel, is neither a return to an old way of thought—the path of fundamentalism whether it is found in Christianity or Islam—nor a blind continuation of the current way which can only propel us faster and farther into the geography of nowhere.

What is called for, and what seems to be emerging, is a third way of thought or a new way of understanding the "amphibian" nature of we creatures who can live in both the world of time and the realm of eternity.

This can only be done by first understanding—or perhaps *remembering*—what it was like to live in a world where the vertical and the horizontal planes of our existence were not so far apart, for I think it is safe to say that for most of human history we amphibian beings have lived in the city of the gods, a place quite unlike the place where our journey to nowhere has brought us in the past few hundred years.

It would, of course, be impossible to unlearn or abandon the modern way of thought that has evolved over the past three hundred and fifty years. We cannot turn back the clock on human learning, even if we wanted to, though that is the method that many conservatives seem to wish to try. Imagining an idealized past, they attempt to deny the changes that have taken place in between. That would be too easy, and not really satisfactory, even if it were possible.

The real task—a most difficult one—is to reunify the premodern and postmodern minds, bringing about a real reconciliation of opposites. To do this, it will be necessary to explain the *premodern* mind in terms that the postmodern mind will find acceptable. That is the task of the remainder of this book.

CHAPTER 5

The Way to Somewhere

IN RECENT YEARS, IT HAS BECOME A MEDICAL COMMONPLACE that the human cardio-vascular system thrives better on a fairly "primitive" diet that is high in fiber and low in animal fats than on the "modern" diet of refined grains and saturated fats. Before the modern era, the human diet consisted primarily of grains and fruits. It still does today in "unadvanced" countries where protein in the form of meat still calls for a huge expenditure of energy in the form of hunting, cattle driving, slaughtering, preserving, etc. Until fairly recent times, the human organism never had to process large quantities of animal fats, and therefore it did not really "learn" to do so at any point in its evolutionary history. The digestive system simply never had to adapt to a high fat, low fiber diet because animal fats were simply not available in large enough quantities to do any harm, and so processing them was not an issue in the selection of which genes were to be passed on. As a result, our bodies do not process fats very well. Too much fat and the arteries begin to clog, too little fiber and the colon gets blocked. The "modern" diets we have chosen are not good for us because they are not the sort of diet which we, as a species, "grew up on." To maintain optimum health, therefore, we are now advised to eat farther down the food chain, to eat, in other words, just as our ancient ancestors did in the days before agri-business and refrigeration. The more "primitive" the diet, the better for our arteries.

Similarly, our bodies do not stay trim without a great deal of physical exercise. We are now advised to spend at least three half-hour periods per week doing fairly vigorous physical activities in order to maintain the fitness of our hearts and arteries and the suppleness of our muscles and joints. In other words, just as in our diet, we are advised to recreate artificial conditions which resemble the lifestyle of our primitive ancestors who, after all, did not fall out of trees into automobiles and modern desk jobs. Since our forebears would have spent large amounts of time every day walking, running, hunting, stretching, gathering, and lifting, so must we set aside time to jog, ride stationary bikes, swim, or otherwise make up for the evolutionary lacks of our modern world. It's either that or we court such diseases of the modern age as heart attacks, colon cancer, hypertension and so on.

Many of these bodily processes are unconscious. Digestion, respiration, heart rate and similar activities of the autonomic nervous system* happen without much, if any, conscious thought or direction on our part. It is obvious to anyone who has tried to maintain a healthy diet or a regular exercise program that one has to remind oneself constantly that this activity is "good for me" because it is easy to forget the connection between diet and clogged arteries. And yet attention must be paid to that subliminal, autonomic level of our existence or our well-being is at risk.

In the same way, we constantly seek to recreate the physical environment of the African savannah on which our species evolved some four and a half million years ago. Most of our early evolutionary history took place in what is today Kenya. It is a place where the average humidity is fairly low and the temperature does not vary much from seventy degrees. In the broad grasslands of modern day Kenya, our ape-like ancestors would have had a large horizon to encircle them and a vast dome of sky to behold above them.

We humans have had to live in that world ever since, even to the point of carrying it with us for the past few million years as we migrated from Africa and settled over virtually the entire planet and moved out beyond it into outer space. Whether we descend to the bottom of the earth's oceans or shoot ourselves outside its atmosphere in space shuttles, we must carry with us in our exploration cannisters the climate of the African savannah on which we evolved or we will not survive. If our body temperature grows too cold, we die from hypothermia; too hot and our body temperature rises too high for us to continue to live. Thus, we insure that the temperature and humidity in sea labs and space labs, not to mention in our homes, is the one we "grew up" with. We are most comfortable, feel most ourselves, when we have a temperature and humidity which reproduces, in effect, the conditions of the African savannah. Any hotter or colder than that and we will turn on air conditioning or build a fire to bring the temperature back to our evolutionary standard. We always strive to remain in our African cradle.

Physically, the human organism is a sort of evolutionary layer cake, with our modern bodies and minds resting atop the buried strata of our evolutionary past much like the geological strata of the earth's crust and core. The organism never quite adapted to modern life and so we must recreate, on a daily basis, our ancient environment. Inside each of us there resides a two million year old human being not very far below the postmodern surface. This two million year old being makes demands on us in terms of food and physical conditions, and its demands must be met or we become "dis-eased." Things get out of balance, the organism does not function properly.

Food, physical conditioning and environment are only the simplest of the demands that this ancient person within us makes. On a more complex level, this creature also has drives and impulses which govern such primitive "instincts" as territoriality, aggression, sexuality, bonding, dominance, and so on. Many of these mechanisms operate below the threshold of consciousness, as, for example, the "space bubble" which each of us requires around our selves to feel at ease. The size of this space bubble varies from culture to culture, but every human being needs to have some personal room around him/herself to feel comfortable. If you don't think so, notice what happens next time someone comes "too close." You'll see that, quite without thinking about it, you back away to a "comfortable" distance.

Ancient physiological systems related to aggression also reside within each of us. To introduce my students to them, I begin a class period early in the semester with a purposely dull patch of lecture guaranteed to put them to sleep. When I am sure all eyes are glazed over, I suddenly push over the large wooden lectern on which I've been leaning. Crash!

The transformation is remarkable. Instantly, with no thought at all, these postmodern men and women are poised and ready with all the ancient flight and fight responses of their primate ancestors. Their eyes flash open, their pupils dilate, their nostrils flare, their muscles grow taut and ready for action. Some of them shout, as if to frighten off a predator. After an initial intake of surprised breath, respiration continues at an increased rate, there's a flush on the skin and the formerly slouched student bodies in front of me are upright and alert. In less than a second, the adrenal system has kicked in and, quite without thinking, postmodern men and women experience their ancestor within, at least that part which resides in the autonomic nervous system.

Since the scientific revolution of the seventeenth century and following, we moderns have largely identified "mind" as only those higher functions of logic, abstract thought and language located in the neocortex and have ignored, largely, the other more "primitive" levels of our brains except when a pathology arises in which case we dispense medicine to "control" the symptoms. Having defined ourselves in the eighteenth century as the "rational animal," we focused on the rational part and denied the animal—which included most of the irrational, messy parts of ourselves that the rational mind gets uncomfortable with.

It is relatively easy for us to admit that the body has some fairly primitive needs. We accept the fact that a simple diet, physical exercise and so on are necessary for survival in the modern world. But it is more difficult to convince a "modern" person that his mind, too, has primitive needs which are as important, if not more important, than the primitive needs of the body. So much has the rational mind inflated its self-importance that it has difficulty admitting even the existence of this primitive mind, much less acknowledging that it has needs that must be met and that if the needs of the primordial mind are not met, then—to continue our analogy with the needs of the physical body—we will begin to experience dysfunction on the psychological and spiritual levels comparable to clogging of the arteries or atrophy of the muscles.

The point I am try to make is this: up until fairly recent times, human beings had a way of acknowledging the deeper levels of their being, of addressing the needs of the most ancient and primitive parts of themselves. A common language existed by which the old and new parts of our brains could communicate with each other. Since the scientific revolution in the West, however, we have thrown aside or forgotten the ancient language and, in the process, have lost touch with some essential, species-specific wisdom without which we may not be able to survive. To pursue the analogy with human digestion and the cardiovascular system a little further, we could say that we have been ignoring the good, high fiber, low fat "nutrition" of the lower levels of our brain in exchange for the high cholesterol fat of the frontal brain. The result has been the hypertense, clogged-up postmodern condition.

There are many names for the lower strata of the human psyche. In the past century, scientists have come up with different labels for this region of deep knowledge which we could say constitutes the human brain's "hardware."

Towards the end of the nineteenth century, anthropologists like Adolf Bastian and James Frazier began collecting stories from various cultures around the world. It was part of the same Romantic tendency that caused the Grimm brothers and others to collect and study folk tales from their own cultures. As they studied these tales, it became clear that certain patterns repeated themselves again and again. Buried beneath the surface variations of tales and myths, they discovered virtually the same ideas, images and patterns of thought occuring in all or nearly all human societies in all or nearly all times or places. This, they theorized, must reflect an underlying structure built-in to the human way of knowing. That is, human knowledge, because it is human, will always take on these distinctive forms. Bastian referred to these underlying forms as *Elementargedanken** or "Elementary ideas," which appear as a sort of "deep form" under a variety of different cultural and ethnic disguises which he called "local ideas" or *Volksgedanken.*

Carl Jung, the Swiss founder of analytical psychology, called these elementary ideas "archetypes,"* by which he meant structures in the unconscious part of the human psyche which, if studied, would reveal the underlying, universal operating mechanisms of the human mind.

Basic to Jung's thought is the idea that the human psyche is composed of a conscious and an unconscious part. The unconscious part is autonomous, largely non-verbal and lies below the level of consciousness. According to Jung, the larger part of the human psyche, by far, is the unconscious. It operates day and night, manifesting itself to us in the form of dreams, daydreams, fantasies, and imagination. It bodies itself forth in works of art and other "inspired" activities. It has found powerful form in religious symbolism and ritual.

Through this region, the libido,* or basic psychological energy, flows towards consciousness. Its movement is governed by an archetype Jung called the Self, often represented as a complete circle, which is both the goal towards which the psychic energy is directed and also its guide, making sure it moves in the proper direction for the growth of the Self.

It is Jung's contention, as it can be ferreted out from his Collected Works, that our primordial human ancestors functioned largely on the level of the unconscious, without the aid—and/or interference—of consciousness. In that state, the Self is more or less in unconscious unity with its environment, existing in a state that anthropologists have identified as a *participation mystique*,* or mystical participation in the larger life of the universe from which the individual feels no separation. As is the case with reptiles and apes and other life forms, the conscious, analytical, divisive frontal brain had not yet established its hegemony as it has in the modern West.

Jung more or less identifies the unconscious with the ancient autonomic nervous system when he writes:

> The unconscious is the psyche that reaches down from the daylight of mentally and morally lucid consciousness into the nervous system that for ages has been known as the sympathetic. This does not govern perception and muscular activity like the cerebrospinal system, and thus control the environment; but, though functioning without sense organs, it maintains the balance of life and, through the mysterious paths of sympathetic excitation, not only gives us knowledge of the innermost life of other beings but also has an inner effect on them. In this sense it is an extremely collective system, the operative basis of all *participation mystique*, whereas the cerebrospinal function reaches its high point in separating off the specific qualities of the ego, and only apprehends surfaces and externals—always through the medium of space. It experiences everything as an out-

side, while the sympathetic system experiences everything as an inside.[1]

In a recent book, Jungian analyst Anthony Stevens outlines the role this ancient self plays in our modern psychological lives, and shows, from a medical and psychological perspective, how important it is to pay heed to its demands.

Each of us, in our growth from the *participation mystique* of infancy to the individuation of adulthood, recapitulates the psychological history of the human species, reliving, as it were, the evolutionary development of the species from its infancy to its fuller, conscious individuation. An infant is, in Jungian terms, all unconsciousness. It lives in "mystical participation." It cannot tell where itself leaves off and anything "other" begins. In this state, it experiences perfect identification with its surroundings. Whatever it touches—its mother, its crib blanket or a bottle nipple—the child does not sense any essential separation between the object and him.

Slowly, a more or less differentiated consciousness begins to evolve out of this primordial state and the child matures and differentiates itself from its environment as its consciousness grows.

Generally, we tend to regard the process of maturation as one level of consciousness *displacing* the previous ones. We may think (mistakenly) of the child outgrowing stages of consciousness and modes of thought much as he outgrows his baby shoes and clothes and gets new ones. Once the higher levels of abstract reasoning and logic make their appearance in the child, we expect him/her to leave behind whatever modes of thought are "childlike." Thus, we all become adults.

But, as Jung demonstrates so well in his works, the primordial levels of the brain are *not* supplanted by new functions any more than the ancient dietary needs of the body are displaced by modern

---

[1]C. G. Jung, "Archetypes of the Collective Unconscious," in *The Collected Works of C. G. Jung.* Princeton: Princeton Univ. Press, 1969. Vol. 9, I, para. 41. For a fuller treatment of this subject, see Anthony Stevens' *The Two-Million Year Old Self,* Houston: Texas A&M Univ. Press, 1993.

diets; the old levels of psyche are merely ignored or driven underground, back into the vast, undifferentiated sea of libido where they continue to exert their titanic energies in spite of all the conscious mind* can do. They make their appearance in dreams, fantasies and, more negatively, in pathologies, for just as physical pathology will result when the primordial needs of the body are shorted, so, too, contended Jung, will psychological or even "spiritual" pathology result when the needs of the primordial mind and soul are thwarted.

What is the nature of this unconscious mind* whose needs we, as a culture, have not fully attended to for perhaps the last three hundred and fifty years? It is quite different from the modern mind we are accustomed to.

First of all, it functions on the level of *participation mystique*, having a total identification with its environment. The "modern" consciousness which evolved from it holds that I and that tree over there are not one and the same thing. Logic says that "A" and "not-A" cannot inhabit the same space at the same time. The unconscious mind knows differently, however, and it can prove it, not by logical argument, but only through experience.

Secondly, the unconscious mind exists mostly outside the realm of normal time. A quick look at your dreams will reveal this. People who are dead come back to life. You find yourself in places you have not been for thirty years. You are child, adult and teenager simultaneously. Clearly this unconscious mind has no sense of sequential time. It operates outside the categories of past, present and future, now and then, and consequently it experiences everything in a perpetual present where the beginning of things and their ends exist simultaneously, where there is no necessary sequence of events and where, if there is any notion of "time" at all, it tends to be circular, arranging events so that they will return eternally. It is this time of no time which the unconscious considers to be "real" time, the time when events and actions achieve a sort of validity they do not have in ordinary clock time. In this, it is clearly related to ritual time where, in the Mass or in repeating the rituals of the elders, one abolishes history and re-enters eternity.

Thirdly, we can say that the unconscious or primordial human mind is ego-less. It does not experience a distinct "I" in the way that our modern western minds do. Since the world and "I" are one in our *participation mystique*, then there is no "I" separate from the world. "I" do not think thoughts, they think me. I do not act on the world, actions act me in the world. The individual ego is fairly irrelevant in this scheme. This is the element of the unconscious mind which makes totemism possible, for if one has no real self, then one can really *be* the crocodile or the deer, not simply identifying the self with the totem animal but actually sharing its existence. The ancient mind does not seem to distinguish between its self and its environment. At the higher levels of religious thought, this makes possible the Upanishads' famous phrase *tat tvam asi*, "thou art that," for there is no ego in the unconscious. What Jung calls the ego could correspond to what we have called the conscious brain which thinks it is in charge. But the ego, the conscious self, is only a fragment of the total life of the Self for, as we've seen, the frontal part of the brain is only, at best, a third of the whole show. To confuse the small ego self with the larger Self is like taking the fingernail for the whole hand.

Finally, the primordial or unconscious mind recognizes as *real* the world which exists below or beyond the world of appearances. The world of matter, which the modern Cartesian mind calls "real," is merely an illusion for it is constantly in flux. Beneath it, accessible to the unconscious mind, is the world of permanence, the world of *mana*, or power and it is to this underlying reality that the unconscious mind responds.

We could briefly outline the differences between these two minds as follows:

Unconscious Mind *(Primordial)*	**Conscious Mind** *(Modern)*
1. mystical participation	1. separation, differentiation
2. eternity	2. time
3. ego-less	3. emphasizes "I," ego-self
4. Real world is the world of *mana* or spirit. Physical world is unreal, illusion.	4. Real world is world of matter. Unquantifiable world of *mana* or spirit must be unreal, illusion.

These two minds attempt to speak to one another in the modern individual. Both are working fairly constantly even if they remain unaware of each other's activities. The unconscious mind does not stop altogether while the conscious mind is working. It continues to observe, send messages, react to what is going on up above on the conscious level. Like digestion, respiration, and the pulse rate, the unconscious mind continues to function without our conscious awareness even as the conscious mind goes about its day-to-day activities. And just as with the body's physical functions, if we ignore the unconscious mind and do not attend to its needs, then we put ourselves at peril. The difficulty is that they do not have a common language and yet they must work together if we are to remain in full mental and spiritual health.

Jung says that the consciousness which we have identified as "modern" arose only about two thousand five hundred years ago with the ancient Greeks and their invention of logic and the rudiments of what we have come to call the scientific worldview. As we outlined in the previous two chapters, it evolved fully during the late Renaissance and then came to dominate the Western mode of thought since the Enlightenment. During the period of its heyday, this "mind" brought tremendous progress in the material world. In medicine, physics, the applied arts and technology, as we've seen, the human species made tremendous strides forward. But all this time, if we accept Jung's model, we have ignored the unconscious self which was there all along, like the heart and kidneys, working as best it could in spite of all we were doing to ignore or deny it.

We could draw the Self as an iceberg, the tip of which is modern consciousness:

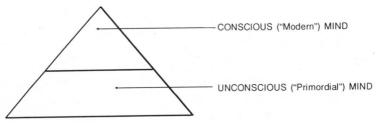

This diagram, however, implies that modern consciousness is somehow superior to or in control of the unconscious mind. More aptly I think, we could see the strata of the Self as existing side by side as follows:

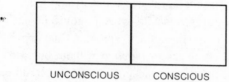

UNCONSCIOUS   CONSCIOUS

Or even as concentric circles or spheres, the modern consciousness surrounding, in a sense, the unconscious mind which constantly threatens to expand its influence outward:

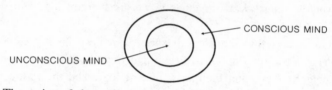

The point of these diagrams is to illustrate that the needs of the primordial unconscious mind exist contemporaneously with the needs of the modern conscious mind, just as ancient and modern needs co-exist in the body.

But we moderns have put a chasm between the conscious and the unconscious self, largely through supression of the unconscious impulses, and the result has been the confusion of the modern world which we have outlined above. For when we return to the feelings of fragmentation, alienation and loss of center that we identified as hall-marks of the "modern" and postmodern attitudes, are not these the feelings that result from an over-reliance on the conscious functions of analysis and logic and from ignoring the unifying functions of the unconscious?

The gift or special talent of the unconscious mind is its marvel-ous ability to connect us to the cosmos, to give us a place in the world and to connect us with our community. These attachments are among the fundamental needs of the human condition, as fundamental as the need for food, water and sleep. These are the needs of the unconscious self which we have learned to ignore much to our mod-ern discomfort and dislocation.

Now, if there is a chasm between the conscious and the unconscious, there must also be (or once have been) a way for these two sorts of "minds" to communicate with one another. Obviously the conservative wisdom of the old brain must have had a way to communicate itself to the lively, inventive, and sometimes dangerous, new modern brain.

What forgotten language is it that allows, and has allowed, us to speak across the chasm? The answer, perhaps, may be found in the ancient language of myth, symbol and ritual, and it is to this near-forgotten language that we now must turn for it is there, along the ancient songlines* of our species, that we may find the thread that will lead us out of the postmodern labyrinth.

CHAPTER 6

The Songlines

IN HIS FINAL BOOK, *THE SONGLINES,*[1] BRITISH AUTHOR BRUCE Chatwin presents a fictionalized account of his encounter with the Songlines* or "Dreaming tracks" of the Australian aborigines. The Songlines are both traditional songs and invisible tracks which crisscross Australia in a complex web. The aborigines believe that in the beginning, in the great Dreaming, legendary beings wandered over the face of the earth "singing out the name of everything that crossed their path—birds, animals, plants, rocks, waterholes."[2] In this way, the world was "sung" into existence. Known as "Footprints of the Ancestors" or "The Way of the Law," the songlines are traditional maps, passed down in musical form through the generations, a sort of mythological Rand McNally by which an aborigine can find his way across a thousand miles of unknown territory simply by singing.

The aborigine who sets out across Australia to "sing up the land," however, is not simply availing himself of a sort of pre-literate road atlas. Equally important, he is also putting himself into the Dreamtime* where, by singing, he actively participates in the ongoing creation of the world. Without continued singing of the Songlines, Chatwin reports, the world would cease to be. Thus, the penalty for forgetting one's own song or for singing it out of order in the great cycle of songs is often death.

In aboriginal society, Chatwin says, ". . . everyone inherited . . . a stretch of the Ancestor's song and the stretch of country over which the song passed. A man's verses were his title deeds to territory. He could lend them to others. He could borrow other verses in return. The one thing he couldn't do was sell or get rid of them."[3]

---

[1] New York: Penguin, 1987.

[2] Ibid., p. 2.

The complexity of the Songlines as \
territories is astonishing. A single song c
languages from one end of the continent to t
ous tribes and kinship groups cross or conver
and, in practice, become markers used to d(
purposes of exogamy* and hunting. These ter.
coincide exactly with modern maps or national   ...u out
by surveyors. A tribal area may have over si.. .undred Dreamings
going through it, with crossover points that form sort of stagecoach
stops. Each "handover point" was dreamed by an ancestor, long before current political boundaries were established by the immigrating
Europeans.

The Songline is nothing less than a spiritual geography laid out
on top of the physical geography of Australia. It unites the past with
the present, and the spirit world with the world of matter. But that's
not all. It is also the source of future generations since each Ancestor,
in his original singing up of the landscape during the Dreamtime, left
a spoor of "life cells" or "spirit children" so that each of his descen-
dants would, in addition to his/her biological father, also have a sort
of spiritual father. The idea is this: one of these "musical sperm" deposited by an ancestor leaves the Songline and enters into a pregnant
woman's body when she steps on that spot. Thus there is a sort of
second, spiritual conception in the already-fertilized womb. This second conception is signaled by the infant's first kick in the womb.
The woman tells the Elders where and when the kick occurred and
the identity of this spirit is determined by the Elders who reserve the
unborn child a place on the appropriate Songline which he will in-
herit and learn as his own piece of this complex spatio-spiritual web.

In this way, generation after generation becomes tied to the
physical and spiritual landscape of Australia in a way that astonishes,
perplexes, awes and mystifies Westerners who simply draw road maps
connecting spaces by the straightest lines possible and consider themselves done with it.

As the melody of the Songline passes rhythmically out of the
innermost self of the singer, however, something more remarkable

---

[3]Ibid., p. 57.

geography happens. Memory fuses with breath and voice
three enter the world together, establishing a powerful imagi-
ative connection among the individual, his community and the cosmic Dreamtime.

One cannot help but be struck here by the similarity between
the aboriginal Songlines and the book of *Genesis* with its creator God
bringing forth the universe through the power of his word, and giving
to Adam the task of naming all the creatures of the earth.

> And out of the ground the Lord God formed every beast of the field,
> and every fowl of the air; and brought them unto Adam to see what
> he would call them: and whatsoever Adam called every living crea-
> ture, that was the name thereof. (Gen. 2:19)

When Eve comes along, she is named in her turn, and throughout the Hebrew and Christian scriptures, the act of naming makes a
thing exist, as though without being called into existence, it could not
fully be. In the Bible, the act of calling thus both indicates what a
thing's essential nature is, and also creates it at one and the same
time. Thus the significance of name changes in the Bible—Avram to
Abraham, Simon to Peter, Saul to Paul, etc. What we call things is
not irrelevant. In the beginning was the word, both for the Aborigine
and the Judaeo-Christian.

The Songlines and the Bible are only two examples of the great
cycles of comosgonic myths that the world's many cultures rely upon
to give them a sense of connectedness. Traditionally, stories, or
myths, have been the means by which humans have linked together
the disparate threads of their lives, and yet, we modern human beings
have more or less wilfully cut ourselves off from stories as a way of
"knowing" about our lives and experience. We call them "mere stories" and do not give them much credit beyond their entertainment
value.

One could stretch the history of this abandoning of the story
back at least to Plato who, in his *Republic*, would have banned poets
and artists from his ideal state because they had nothing of practical
value to offer the citizens except their poetic "lies." For our purposes, however, we need go no further back than the Scientific Revolution of the seventeenth century when, as noted above, Western rationalism rather definitively split knowing into two distinct modes,

the new scientific mode and, for lack of a better term, the older "poetic" one. To the newer mode belong the impressive and powerful tools of logic and the undeniable "progress" in the learned and applied arts that has occurred over the past three hundred years. To the older mode belongs the traditional world of poetry, the arts and religion—all those modes of being and thinking that relied upon narrative* rather than mathematics and logic for their coherence.

It is not surprising to find, as analyst Marie Louise von Franz points out, that up until about the middle of the seventeenth century the stories we call "fairy tales" were told to adults by adults. After that time, however, they became "mere" children's fare, unworthy of serious, i.e. "adult," attention which thenceforth would be directed towards logic, science and technology. Eventually, even the Bible joined the company of mere narrative superstition when its truths could not be squared with *the* truth we had learned from scientific thought.

In *The Postmodern Condition*, Lyotard points out, rightly I think, that we have lost the narrative as a form of knowledge. Narrative, says Lyotard, is the means by which a culture passes on the sort of knowledge that the French call *savoir*, as distinguished from *connaissance*. While *connaissance* ("book-learning") refers to knowledge which may be declared either true or false, *savoir*, includes such things as know-how (*savoir-faire*), and "knowing how" in the sense of competence, judgment, aesthetics, values and evaluation. He writes, ". . . [*savoir*] coincides with an extensive array of competence building measures and the only form embedded in a subject constituted by the various areas of competence composing it."[4]

This form of knowledge involves mental processes quite different from those involved in the acquiring of simple *connaissance*. One might call the skills involved "global" in that they involve the whole organism, not just the higher levels of the brain, in the learning process. It's a different *kind* of knowing.

In the case of the Songlines, for example, a singer learns many things at once as he memorizes his section of the Songline. He learns a sort of road map across Australia, of course, but he is also learning how to sing, how to participate rhythmically in the life of the tribe, how to relate himself to the land, to the non-tribe, to history, to pre-history, to the animal and geological realm, and finally to eternity. Once learned, the song, woven from memory, larynx, sound and sight, constitutes a kind of knowledge far more deeply interfused in the various layers of the self than mere "book learning." One learns it, as the old expression has it, "by heart," and it resists falsification. If someone says that, logically speaking, no crocodile could possibily have been involved in the creation of crocodile mountain, he has missed the point. And yet, this is exactly what the "scientific" mind does in the face of mythological truths. Of the narrative form of knowledge, it says, "Yes, once in our infancy we could believe such things that way, but now we are beyond that kind of belief, that kind of knowing."

And yet, the rich and complex narrative form of knowledge is the form in which important information has been transmitted from one generation to the next in human cultures as far back as we can tell.

If we examine the earliest evidences of human cult activity, the cave burials in central Europe and Eurasia from about 75,000 B.P., we will find the presence already of a sort of "narrative" that must have enabled our ancestors to understand the experience of death. That narrative must have gone something like this: a strange thing has happened to our fellow. He has gone cold and the breath has passed from his body. Something of what he was has gone away. The sun, too, leaves us in cold and darkness, yet daily it returns at the other end of the earth. Once, like the sun at night, our fellow did not exist, then he was born. He passed among us like the sun but now is gone. Perhaps his going is like his coming, back into the earth as he came from his mother. Perhaps he is being born again, in some other place, or perhaps, like the sun, he is journeying, so we should leave tools, food, clothing to accompany him wherever he may be and leave him here as if the end of his life were a beginning of another life in some other place.

Now, no "proof" is possible for the accuracy of the above story, but the essential point is this—in spite of its lack of factual reference, this sort of narrative, more than any other form of knowledge, made life in the face of death possible for thousands of generations of our ancestors. More than any other way of knowing, this sort of story has enabled us to live with a sense of *meaning* in an otherwise meaningless universe.

As far as I know, after some twenty years of reading anthropological and psychological literature, no human population anywhere has ever been found which did not possess, in at least a rudimentary form, stories and myths which accounted for their existence, their social patterns, and their relationships with such cosmic matters as life, death, and the afterlife. It is only within the past couple of hundred years in Western intellectual history that we have had the *hybris* to think that we may do without these "mere" stories, or that their form of knowledge has been superceded by a new and better form: scientific thought, which renders them obsolete or irrelevant.

An old Zen saying has it that you cannot travel south if your wagon is pointed north. Could it be that the widespread sense that life in the postmodern world has become meaningless stems from the fact that some time ago we jettisoned the story as a means of experiencing meaning and have been searching for it ever since in the wrong way? Perhaps we postmoderns have been searching in the wrong places for something that was there all along. Lyotard says as much when he writes, "Lamenting the 'loss of meaning' in postmodernity boils down to mourning the fact that knowledge is no longer principally narrative."[5]

It is remarkable to me that wherever we turn in human history—save the present—we find the deepest knowledge of the tribe expressed in the narrative mode. Turn whichever way we choose—except towards ourselves—we cannot avoid the conclusion that most human beings in most times and most places have found in the narrative form some type of knowledge that was indispensable for existence. We are forced to conclude, I think, that storytelling, in some form or another, seems to have some sort of survival value for the species.

Fascinating speculation in this direction comes from maverick anthropologist Robin Fox who builds on P. D. MacLean's triune con-

---

[5]Ibid., p. 26.

cept of the brain. Briefly, MacLean's idea is this: the human animal has a hierarchically organized brain consisting of the old reptilian brain,* the old mammalian* and the distinctly human new mammalian brain* or neocortex.* Each of these levels of the triune brain* has its disinct mode of operation and its distinct function in maintaining the overall health of the organism. Each of the three brains "has its own peculiar form of subjectivity and its own intelligence, its own sense of time and space, and its own memory, motor and other functions."[6]

The reptilian brain, buried deep within us, seems intimately involved in certain stereotyped behaviors such as territoriality, certain types of "display" behavior, hunting, homing, mating, breeding, imprinting, forming social hierarchies and even selecting leaders.[7]

This part of the human brain, being very ancient, is highly conservative. It is programmed for survival. Like the reptiles for which it is named, it possesses a sort of "wisdom" about what is needed to get along in this world's harsh conditions at least long enough to pass its genes along to the next generation.

The next level of brain which MacLean posits is the old mammalian brain or limbic system.* This type of brain, found commonly in mammals such as rabbits, cats, and monkeys, as well as in humans, concerns itself with "fighting, feeding and self-protection." It also has a strong connection to the hypothalamus "which plays a basic role in integrating emotional expression" in human beings.[8] It also is the location of feeling states which are "conducive to sociability and other preliminaries of copulation and reproduction." These functions of the limbic system—the famous four "F's" of feeding,

---

[6]Paul D. MacLean, *The Triune Concept of Brain and Behavior.* T. J. Boag and D. Campbell, eds. Toronto: Univ. of Toronto Press, 1973. p. 8.

[7]On this last point consider the odd but well-known fact that virtually all presidents of the United States have been above average height for their generations, then consider that among primates and many other species dominance and power hierarchies are determined by height or by rituals in which head and shoulder movements are exaggerated to give the impression of greater height. Could it be that we select our leaders not by their positions on the issues but on our ape-like prejudice to grant dominance to the tall?

[8]MacLean. p. 12.

fighting, feeling and fornication—we share with other mammals, and ethnobiologists have found no end of similarities between human be- havior in these areas and the behavior of other animals who share with us this level of brain. This should not surprise us, given the fact that until only a few million years ago we *were* apes or at least more ape-like. But then about four and half million years ago, a re- markable leap in evolution took place.

For some rather obvious reasons, the development of a frontal lobe which contained such higher mental functions as speech and ab- stract thought gave our ancestors a survival advantage over their pri- mate neighbors. Laid on top of the primitive levels of brain which had been successfully surviving for some millions of years, this neo- cortex added a new dimension of problem solving, even to the extent of being able to anticipate problems that had not yet occurred. There is no question that evolution favored the frontal lobes. As an adapta- tion mechanism, it was extraordinarily successful. The rapid expan- sion of cranial size indicates the evolutionary advantage of such an adaptation.

However, we can see that there is a distinct design problem with this neocortical development. While it is a marvelous biological innovation, the neocortex was laid on top of two far older, more primitive levels of brain. The analogy might be to putting a turbo- charger on the engine of a Model T. Distinct clashes of "style" in- evitably arise between the flashy new brain and the time-tested, dura- ble, reliable, if somewhat backward-looking, old mammalian and rep- tilian brains. Perhaps the most severe problem is that this new brain and the old brains do not share a common language.

While the new brain communicates with itself primarily through language and possesses the verbal centers of the brain, the old brains are decidedly non-verbal. As MacLean succinctly puts it, "the neural machinery does not exist for the reptilian and limbic brains to com- municate in verbal terms." The essential difficulty, says MacLean, is that "our neocortex is all out of step with our animal brains."[9]

Without getting too deep into the neurology and physiology of the matter, we can state the problem this way—the highly verbal, for-

---

[9]Ibid., pp. 18-19.

ward-thinking, adaptable, problem-solving part of our brain cannot communicate easily with the deeply buried, ritualistic, repetitive, traditional, even "conservative" part.

A strange creature this, nearly schizoid by nature. One thinks of cases where the left and right hemispheres of the brain have been separated by a commissurotomy* and one hemisphere can identify an object by its picture but cannot name its name while the other hemisphere knows the name but cannot pick up the object. If what MacLean says is true, then this bizarre state is really nothing more than a mirror of the normal state of the human mind in which the older, non-verbal levels share no common language with the highly verbal frontal brain.

Clearly, it would be advantageous to the organism for all three brains to be integrated, but how can this be accomplished when the gap between them seems so extraordinarily wide?

Enter the dreamers.

In his fascinating essay "The Passionate Mind: Brain, Dreams, Memory, Evolution, and Social Categories," Robin Fox lays a groundwork for finally re-synthesizing the two human modes of knowing.[10]

Recent studies have shown that the regions of the brain used in processing information into long-term memory are largely the so-called limbic areas or limbic system, corresponding to the area MacLean has called the "old mammalian" brain. These regions and the organs in them—the hippocampus, thalamus, and hypothalamus—are also intimately connected to the experiencing of emotions.

According to Fox and others, REM sleep (i.e. dreaming), is extremely important in moving information through the proper "neuronal gates" to get it into long-term memory. Recent studies indicate that dream deprivation interferes with memory retention. Subjects deprived of dreaming sleep have more difficulty remembering learned tasks and information than those allowed to "dream" them into memory.

"So one conclusion is obvious," Fox writes

---

[10] In *The Search for Society: Quest for a Biosocial Science and Morality.* New Brunswick, NJ: Rutgers Univ. Press, 1989.

whatever else dreams are doing, they are serving as a processing system for memory; and this processing system is located in the hippocampus and its limbic connections.[11]

The process for real long-term memory is terribly time-consuming, but once established in the long-term memory, information remains fixed. Fox states:

> . . . for anything to enter long-term memory, it has to be processed (i.e. dreamed) for at least three years in some form or other. Experiments have shown that during this process the synapses—connections between neurons that carry the 'information'—actually grow and harden into habitual pathways thus facilitating the rapid processing of memory.[12]

The implications of this research for the "postmodern" dilemma are enormous, for if these conclusions about dreaming—and by extension those "dreamlike" states of fantasy, active imagination, artistic creation and ritual participation—are correct, then in jettisoning the dream, mythology and ritual, we have cut ourselves off from an important, perhaps the most important, means we have for insuring our survival as a species.

It is worth quoting Fox at length here:

> We can only speculate here, but it does seem that what is happening in REM sleep for animals at least[13] is that current information, blocked from the hippocampus and the limbic circuit during waking, is allowed in there during sleep to be 'matched' against those wired-in survival behaviors that are the species' ethogram—its record, if you like, of successful adaptive behavior. If they are 'passed' as being relevant, then they are shunted on through the limbic system to be . . . 'stamped in' to the long-term memory, and eventually stored in the neocortex. . . . Without this information the neocortex could not perform its essential function of assessing experience in order to make plans and goals for future action.[14]

---

[11]Fox, *op. cit.*, p. 179.

[12]Ibid.

[13]Fox wrote this before studies on humans conducted in 1992 which showed similar results in people.

[14]Ibid., p. 179.

Properly understood, this quote tells us that we cannot underestimate the importance of dreaming and dreamlike activity to the successful functioning of human beings.[15] Dreams, which are highly visual and sensate, seem to serve as the common language which translates, as it were, the intellectual, verbal information of the neo-mammalian brain into a symbolic form that the non-verbal reptilian and old mammalian brains can understand. Thus, the forward-looking Promethean neo-cortex has its plans and experiences checked by the more ancient and conservative part of the brain with its accumulated survival wisdom of several million years.

Is it any wonder that we find in human history and literature so much stress laid on the predictive nature of dreams?

In the Bible we see it again and again, most notably in the story of Joseph:

> And Pharaoh said unto Joseph, 'I have dreamed a dream, and there is none that can interpret it: and I have heard say of thee that thou canst understand a dream to interpret it.' (Gen. 41:15-16)

In Shakespeare as well the tradition of the importance of paying attention to dreams is emphasized:

> Calpurnia, my wife, stays me at home.
> She dreamt tonight she saw my statue,
> Which like a fountain with a hundred spouts
> Did run pure blood, and many lusty Romans
> Came smiling and did bathe their hands in it.
> And these does she apply for warnings and portents
> Of evils imminent, and on her knee
> Hath begged that I will stay at home today.
> *(Julius Caesar*, II, ii, 75-82)[16]

---

[15]Note: I am taking some liberties here with Fox in equating dreaming and other "dreamlike" activities such as art, music and ritual, but I hope to show below that such connections are not far-fetched.

[16]Unfortunately for Caesar, Decius responds like the rational forebrain and says, ". . . it were a mock/Apt to be rendered for someone to say 'Break up the Senate till another time/When Caesar's wife shall meet with better dreams." (II, ii, 96-8) This was not the first, nor the last time, that the clear message of dream was thought too curious to be considered.

Perhaps Calpurnia is not so much predicting the future here as comparing recent events at the Capitol with ancient instincts for survival. The dream is the gateway through which such messages pass back and forth.

As Fox writes, dreaming probably evolved as "a *selective processing device* that enabled recent memories to be evaluated against the 'phyletic' memories of the species" in order to give them "time in which to be so processed and evaluated."[17]

In devaluing dreams as "mere" dreams, modern humans have cut themselves off from perhaps one of the most powerful tools available to the species for valuating their experiences, for the rational, logical, materialistic side of us, if allowed to run unchecked, is capable of quite a bit of mischief, inventing nuclear bombs, clearing rain forests, making species go extinct, etc. So it runs its heedless ways. Meanwhile, the non-verbal, highly emotional limbic system, geared as it is towards continued survival, cries out "Stop!" but goes unheard because its dream messages are ignored or written off as the random firing of neurons or as the result of a bit of indigestion.

Freud is often credited with having "discovered" the importance of dreams in our century, but he no more discovered dreams than Columbus discovered the Native Americans who, from their point of view, were always there. So with dreams. From the Bible through Shakespeare they served as guides, omens and predictions. Some societies, like the Senoj have built elaborate social structures around them. Only our society, except for psychoanalysts and analytical psychologists, has felt capable of doing without them. Imagine a modern head of state saying he/she was going to determine policy with the aid of dreams, and watch a politician drop from the sky like a falling star.[18]

Now, one fascinating aspect of the dream that Fox does not mention but that we have to bring out here is that the dream, in humans anyway, most often has a *narrative* form. It only takes a

---

[17]Fox, p. 181.

[18]One need only remember the uproar and ridicule at the end of the Reagan administration when it was revealed that Nancy Reagan regularly consulted an astrologer and used her advice to counsel the president on policy.

moment's reflection to see this. In recalling our dreams we most often see them as little dramas in which we participate as we sleep. In retrospect, they are experienced as having a beginning a middle and an end, a certain plot ("first this happened and then this"). They have settings, subplots, character developments and, occasionally, dialogue. Things *happen* in dreams in a narrative mode. And since the dream is not controlled by consciousness, then what we have in the dream is a sort of baseline operating mode of the human brain. That is, left to its own devices, without the interference of the analytical part of the forebrain, the mind seems spontaneously to take to the narrative form in order to work out its agenda. As James Hillman succinctly puts it, in italics to emphasize the crucial importance of his point:

> . . . *if the dream is psychic nature per se, unconditioned, spontaneous, primary, and this psychic nature can show a dramatic structure, then the nature of the mind is poetic.* To go the root of human ontology, its truth, essence and nature, one must move in the fictional mode and used poetic tools.[19]

And now, with this as an operating assumption, we are ready to take on the postmodern dilemma.

In his thought-provoking—and therefore controversial—works, maverick anthropologist Robin Fox suggests something like the following: myth, storytelling and ritual—indeed all those things that we might lump together under the name "culture"—provide a sort of middle-level language which is understandable, like dreams, by all the various levels of our tri-partite brain. The dream-like form of narrative, ritual and the arts acts as a sort of pidgin English or Esperanto which is both language and yet not language, both the product of the neocortex and yet also of the deeper, non-verbal levels of the human brain. In the symbolic arts (including religious ritual), we have invented a means of bridging the gaps among the three levels of our complex brain in the same way, and perhaps for the same purposes, as dreams do at night. The crucial difference is that while dreams appear to happen spontaneously, without conscious control, in the arts and ritual, consciousness, at least in the beginning, quite often initi-

---

[19] James Hillman, *Healing Fiction*. Barrytown, NY: Station Hill Press, 1983. p. 37.

ates the process. In other words, while dreams seem to come from the unconscious to the conscious mind, occurring during sleep when consciousness is "turned off," ritual, art and myth reverse the process so that the dialogue may be initiated by consciousness.

It is, perhaps, like two old friends who sit down for coffee. Sometimes one starts the conversation, sometimes the other, but once the conversation is going it is difficult to tell or remember who began it. Maybe it is even irrelevant because the important thing is that dialogue is taking place.

The survival advantage to the species of such a symbolic pidgin language is obvious—the neocortex, which seems to have evolved as a present and future problem solver, could use the symbolic language to check itself against the ancient survival knowledge of the more conservative deeper levels of the brain. To hearken back to the horizontal vs. vertical axes of our discussion in Chapter Two, the new mammalian brain which acts primarily in the horizontal realm of history could periodically check its plans and activities against the vertical axis of meaning and eternity.

In the ritual, in the telling of the myth, in the rhythmic beating of the drums, in painting on the cave wall, we enter the gap between the brains in order to measure our present strategies against our ancient wisdom. When the two are in accord, then we may be reasonably certain that any new course of action will benefit the whole organism and ensure the survival of the species. When the two are out of accord, elaborate steps must be taken to bring them back into unity.

And so, in the "nutshell" of the human brain, we find the source of our postmodern dilemma. The very success—even triumph—of the frontal brain along the horizontal axis has led us to believe that it is not necessary to check anymore with the more ancient and tested part of us. For the past three hundred and fifty years or so, we in the West have increasingly ignored our ancient dialogue partner. The result, as we have seen, has been a life wildly out of control, with human animals acting in ways that threaten their very survival as a species, polluting their own drinking water and the air they breathe, degrading the ozone layer that protects them and making weapons that are now literally able to end our existence as a species. Willfully jettisoning our ancient stories and traditions, we cut ourselves off from ancient circadian rhythms, and now we wonder, if we stop to think about it at all, how we got ourselves into the postmodern pickle we find ourselves in.

Symbolic activity, in all its various forms, seems to be the means by which human beings have traditionally connected the microcosm of the self with the macrocosm of the universe at large. In symbolizing, we created a sort of mesocosm, or middle world, which provided the connection. In the terms we have been using, the symbol was the pidgin English which allowed the non-verbal and verbal parts of the brain to communicate. Through painting, sacred stories, icons, ritual dances, masks, and other symbolic expressions, the separation between the various parts of the self could be abolished and one could experience the primordial unity of all things.

Myth and ritual—the sacred story and its enactment—are the twin ladders by which human consciousness has traditionally abolished separation between the new and old, the inner and outer, and thus scaled the vertical axis of meaning. For tens of thousands of years, humans have used their rites and myths to bridge the gap between the sacred timeless truths of the old brain and the profane realities of the new and thereby have experienced a sense of belonging, place and order. For millenia, myth and ritual have given us access to the Great Time, the time outside history, and functioned as examples or models for how we are to get on in the horizontal world of time.

When the myth is acted out in ritual, whether in a ritual dance or the Christian Eucharist, we enter the primordial time where all distinctions between past, present and future, me and them, me and it, are abolished, and the story or rite reaffirms the basic insight of the unconscious mind which is that all is one, *tat tvam asi*. For the myth, passed down from generation to generation and polished along the way to a sort of archetypal brightness, embodies an impersonal, pre-rational mode of thought expressing impersonal, pre-rational realities without which we human beings have never tried before to survive. As Joseph Campbell points out, myths, far from being falsehoods, express absolute *truths* that may be experienced imaginatively but which defy logical articulation. The reason they may defy logic is that the "logic" they must satisfy is the non-verbal, pre-rational logic of the deepest part of the central nervous system.

Symbolic activity provides us a way to temporarily escape the horizontal world of fragmentation and time and to enter the vertical realm of connectedness and meaning. Its "once upon a time" character allows us to enter the realm that Eliade calls *ab illo tempore*, the time of origins, the time outside time where eternal, pre-human verities hold sway. Is it too much to suggest at this point that the "place" we enter in myth and ritual is the ancient brain? Is it too much to say that in the tales of creation and heroes one finds modelled the dynamic tension that must exist between the conscious and unconscious minds? Is the story of the hero conquering the dragon or bringing life out of the jaws of death, a dramatization of the journey of the conscious self into the depths of the unconscious from which he/she reemerges energized, reconnected and whole? The answers to these questions should seem obvious now. In symbolic activity like storytelling and ritual, we experience the proper relationship between the conscious and unconscious: the conscious ego learns not to exclude the unconscious self and at the same time learns how to relate to the unconscious in such a way that it is not overwhelmed by the tremendous tendency of the unconscious to level all things out.

It is in the dynamic and dramatic tension of the myth and ritual that we experience how the symbolic world operates to link together the vertical and horizontal realms of our selves. Thus story and rite serve to bridge the horizontal and vertical and so to unify the two paradoxically different sides of the self. The archetypes are the symbolic language in which this dialogue takes place. The symbol is the means by which the autonomous, impersonal unconscious communicates with consciousness, dramatizes its imbalances and suggests corrective measures.

And yet today we live out of touch with stories and ritual rhythms. Though our world, paradoxically, is filled with stories—on TV, film and radio—we do not know or tell the "big," i.e. archetypal, stories anymore. If we tell them at all, we tell them to children or encounter them as quaint tales related by anthropologists to show off how primitive their subjects are. Likewise, our great collective rites, such as Superbowl Sunday or Inauguration Day, tend to be purely secular.

When the idea is proposed that the cure for the modern and post-modern malaise of fragmentation and alienation is to be found in the story and ritual, the idea at first seems inadequate. In his seminal *The Postmodern Condition*, Jean-Francois Lyotard declares the Narrative as an outmoded form of knowledge, one not compatible with computers and other modern methods of information transmission. In a fragmented world, contends Lyotard, the narrative cannot be a way to truth for the narrative, even less than scientific knowledge, can have no absolute authority as truth. But, then, he concedes, science can have no authority either. And so, in his analysis, the postmodern world is reduced to competing texts which may comment on each other but which may not bear any relation to anything absolute outside themselves. Lyotard's unarguable logic once again deprives modern man of the one source of order and sense that has never let him down, and, like a character in a Samuel Beckett play, he says there is "Nothing to be done." This, it seems to me, is the very definition of the postmodern condition.

But what if the competing texts, far from contradicting each other, actually tell the *same* story. What if beneath the surface differences between the stories and rites from various cultures there is a deeper form which expresses universal human realities? Then, far from a postmodern Babel, we would find unity where there had been fragmentation, peace where there had been confusion, and belonging where there had been alienation.

The postmodern world we live in seems, at first glance, to be so different from ages past that we must abandon any hope of ever regaining the sense of cohesion that must have belonged to previous eras, and yet, as philosopher William Barrett pointed out in *The Illusion of Technique*,[20] people in the contemporary world are not *really* facing any problems which human beings have not faced before. The essential human conditions of birth, suffering, life and death remain unchanged. There may be some change in degree and certainly this postmodern world *looks* different from any other time in human history. But life, after all, was always filled with suffering and confusion. Many times in history—the Black Death in fourteenth-century Europe for one instance—humans have faced mass extinction. Living

---

[20]Garden City, NY: Anchor Books, 1979.

on this planet has, in a sense, always been a precarious proposition. So what really makes the current period so different, says Barrett, is not the problems we face, but the way in which we are facing them:

> The literature of the twentieth century is largely a lamentation for ourselves as victims. And in nothing are we more victims than this: that we have to cope with the same life as humankind in the past but without its most potent means of doing so.[21]

For the first time, he says, human beings are attempting to solve ultimate problems without the benefit of the single source which has, over the millenia, proved effective in reconciling all of life's oppositions—that is, without religion or the spiritual impulse which has found its expression in the sacred stories of world mythology.

Somehow we must find our way back to the old verities. The bad news is that we have so abandoned the old ways of storytelling and rite that we may feel we have lost the knack. The good news is that the ancient world to which we must return does not lie outside us in some inaccessible realm, but it is deep within our own selves and speaks to us continually, if only we can remember how to listen. It is still within our grasp.

The answer to the postmodern dilemma, I believe, is to be found in the place where the answers to life's dilemmas have always been found, in the deep forms or archetypes which reside in the unconscious mind and which strive, even in the midst of the postmodern world, to find articulation. Perhaps by closer examination of the deep form of ancient myths, we can find our way out of the postmodern labyrinth. Finding the road will not be easy but, as Barrett notes, there is a way:

> We cannot will back a faith that has been lost. We shall have to live back into that way of being in whose ambience the religious once drew breath. We shall have to find ourselves within nature before God is able to find us.[22]

And that is the subject to which we shall next turn.

---

[21]Ibid., p. 374.

[22]Ibid., p. 374.

CHAPTER 7

Finding One's Self
in the Postmodern World

IN ONE OF HIS LETTERS, PLUTARCH (46?-120? A.D.) RECOUNTS a discussion held among several travellers to the famous oracle at Delphi. Their topic was "The Passing of the Oracles," a subject in which Plutarch, himself a priest at Delphi, had a keen interest.

Apparently, in the first century A.D., the ancient oracles around the Mediterranean basin fell curiously silent. Ammon in Egypt and Delphi in Greece had ceased sending messages to pilgrims and, recounts Plutarch, " . . .we see the decline of oracles in this country, or rather, the complete disappearance of all but one or two."[1] Silence had descended on the ancient oracles "just as if they were streams of water and a great drought of prophecy had spread over the land."[2]

The travellers inquire among themselves as to the reasons for the drying up of the once-bounteous oracles, and their discussion, oddly, sounds much like the discussions of the death of God in the twentieth century. People are no longer concerned, the cynic Didymus suggests, with the great questions worthy of the gods. Instead, they come asking the wrong questions, questions about fortune telling, treasure hunting, etc., and the gods have grown angry and silent. Others, less jaded, confess they are simply at a loss to explain the curious withdrawal of the gods' voices from among men. Plutarch's description of the state of affairs might well apply to the state of religion in today's churches:

---

[1] "The Passing of the Oracles" in *Plutarch: Selected Lives and Essays*, Louis Ropes Loomis, tr. Rosalyn, NY: Walter J. Black, Inc, 1951. p. 395.
[2] Ibid.

> In some [of the oracles] there lingers only a feeble and hazy remnant of irrational impulse as a faint survival, but others have a great deal of it, hard to suppress. Traces and symbols of all these things are preserved and kept alive in many places, scattered here and there through sacrifices and ceremonies and myths . . .[3]

Reading Plutarch's letter, one gets the impression of a falling off of energy, as if the ancient religions were afflicted with an enervation or spiritual neurasthenia.* A once thriving mythology now lies in shards and those alive can only scratch their heads in bewilderment.

One of the discussants, Philip, tells of a story current at the time that might be relevant to our own postmodern condition. It seems there was a ship full of people passing Paxi, a small island in a cluster of islands known as the Echinades off the west coast of Greece. As they sailed by, the wind strangely died and suddenly a loud voice came from the island calling out the name of Thamus, an Egyptian pilot on board. The voice called twice but Thamus was too shocked to answer. At the third summons, however, he replied. The invisible caller from the shore then delivered his message: "When you are opposite Palodes proclaim that Great Pan is dead!"

After much debate, it was decided that Thamus should fulfill the request, but only if the sea were calm as they passed the second island. The sea being still, Thamus stood on the stern and shouted, "Great Pan is Dead!" and immediately there arose from the island the sound of a multitude of voices moaning in sorrow and astonishment. This remarkable story spread quickly through the Roman empire, reaching even the ears of Tiberius Caesar who ordered an inquiry into it.

"Great Pan is Dead!"

The early Christians took the cry as an omen of the passing of paganism in the face of Christianity, and indeed, from an historical perspective, we can see that Pan and paganism were in their death throes, about to be replaced by the rising sun of the Christian mythos, then beginning its spread through the empire.

---

[3]Ibid., p. 401.

In our own time, some would say, we are living through a passing of the Christian oracle. As it had once supplanted the ancient Greek gods and goddesses, so it, in its turn, has lost its energy and vitality and is on the wane. It has been one of the great themes of modern art and philosophy, from Nietszche's proclamation of God's death through the "absence of God" theme in Bergman's films and Shusako Endo's Christian novels. Nearly everywhere in the Western world there is the sense that the age of miracles is past and that God, today, speaks to mankind *differently* than he did in the past, which may be another way of saying that we feel he is not speaking to us at all.

The magnificent cathedrals of Europe, which were erected in great spasms of religious enthusiasm several hundred years ago, are now mostly tourist spots; the guides are art historians rather than practicing believers. One goes to them seeking "culture" rather than salvation, and buys postcards instead of relics.

In a remarkably perceptive poem, English poet Philip Larkin paints the portrait of postmodern man as a tourist in the land of the holy, one so out of touch with his own *mythos* that he can identify the sanctuary only as "the holy end" and is not quite sure of how this old building once functioned.

Church Going

Once I am sure there's nothing going on
I step inside, letting the door thud shut.
Another church: matting, seats and stone,
And little books; sprawlings of flowers, cut
For Sunday, brownish now; some brass and stuff
Up at the holy end; the small neat organ;
And a tense, musty, unignorable silence,
Brewed God knows how long. Hatless, I take off
My cycle-clips in awkward reverence,

Move forward, run my hand around the font.
From where I stand, the roof looks almost new—
Cleaned or restored? Someone would know, I don't.
Mounting the lectern, I peruse a few
Hectoring large-scale verses, and pronounce

'Here endeth' much more loudly than I'd meant.
The echoes snigger briefly. Back at the door
I sign the book, donate an Irish sixpence,
Reflect the place was not worth stopping for.[4]

There is the same poignancy here that one reads in Plutarch, the same sense of being adrift in a setting that once was charged with meaning but that, of late, has become flat and irrelevant, worth only a passing glance and an Irish sixpence. Like Stonehenge or the Acropolis or the great pyramids of Egypt, the Christian churches which were once so inextricably bound up in the psychological and emotional life of the West now seem to many to be quaint and out of touch with modern realities.

The reasons for this feeling may be twofold: first of all, as outlined above, about three hundred and fifty years ago, the scientific worldview of the West banned non-physical realities from its worldview. Consequently, the image and influence of God dwindled as the rites and scriptures of the Christian West seemed less and less relevant to the day-to-day lives people lived in the increasingly "modern" industrialized and post-industrial world.

As a consequence of this development, we might also say that the ancient stories in their traditional form became inadequate to explain the postmodern realities. That is, the idiom of traditional religion ceased to speak to the changed world in a meaningful way, and so, as happened when history outran the ancient pagan gods, the oracles of Christianity fell silent as those at Delphi did before them.

We find this line of thinking somewhat shocking. It is unsettling to think that the fixed and eternal truths of Christianity might be no more than culturally determined metaphors that have had a life cycle of a couple of thousand years and now are losing, or have already lost, their energy.

Great Pan may die, yes. Zeus, Athena, Tiamat, Marduk, Ishtar, Quetzalcoatl—all these gods arose, produced flourishing civilizations in their names and then died out after a run of a couple of thousand years. But somehow, we believed, Christianity and the culture and

---

[4]Philip Larkin, "Church Going," in *The Norton Anthology of Modern Poetry.* New York: W.W. Norton, 1973. p. 1015.

civilization that grew out of it ought to be immune to the historical processes that carried the other gods away.

And it is not only Christianity that seems to be fading. One could say that the oracles are passing worldwide, wherever the modern and postmodern industrialized and post-industrialized mindset has extended its hegemony. History marches on and mythology lags behind. Oracles have come and gone before, so why should our age be different?

As Joseph Campbell traces the history of world mythology in his four-volume work *The Masks of God* and in his uncompleted *Historical Atlas of World Mythology,* there seem already to have been two great ages of world mythology. The first, already functioning by 20,000 B.C., was the way of the animal powers in which hunting societies expressed belief in theriomorphic* (animal-shaped) gods in ritual and art like the famous cave paintings at Lascaux. These hunting myths lasted some eleven thousand years before they were displaced by the second great mythic cycle, the cycle of the grain goddesses and gods[5] which occurred when there was a major shift in the technology by which people procured food, between 9,500 B.C. and 3,500 B.C. The new technology called forth, as it were, a new mythological context. With the coming of stable crop agriculture in the Middle East, the major mythological motifs shifted from the willing victim motif of the hunters to the sacrificial animal of the agricultural societies. The great grain mythologies—of which the mythos surrounding Jesus is one example ("Take and eat this bread for this is my body")—were closely tied to the primarily agricultural life that most people led until the past one hundred years or so.

In this most recent period (1850-present), however, the conditions of life have changed so radically that some are saying that the old grain mythologies are no longer adequate to fulfill the psychological and spiritual needs of modern and postmodern life. New metaphors must be found, they say, and just as Christianity supplanted the once-flourishing gods of Rome, Greece and Egypt, it

---

[5]It is true that theriomorphic mythologies still hold sway among tribes who have not yet developed agriculture, but there merely proves the point that mythology often follows technology, as will be discussed below. The fact that several mythic styles overlap in human history does not take away from the general validity of the argument.

must, in its turn, yield to historical forces as a new, as-yet-unformed mythology takes its place.

Conservatives in this country are horrified at this idea. They say that the solution to the postmodern dilemma is to return to old values, as though it were possible simply to turn back the clock to a time that, inevitably, is seen as simpler and better. From right-wing politicians and fundamentalist pulpits we hear calls for the "old time religion," for a return to Christian values in America's schools, and so on. All this as though the world were the same world as existed prior to "modernism" with its increased pace, alienation and fragmentation.

This call for a rigid and strict return to "old ways" strikes some, including me, as a form of intellectual Luddism.* The Luddites, you will remember, tried to sabotage the Industrial Revolution by destroying machinery in the new factories of England in order to preserve the centuries old agrarian way of life that was quickly being displanted. It was a rather noble, if futile, enterprise for historical change occurred in spite of all they could do. It is the nature of time to move on.

The mythologies which today dominate the world stage—Judaism, Christianity, Islam, Buddhism, Hinduism, Taoism—came into existence or found their current form during the Axial Age,* that remarkable twelve hundred year period between about 600 B.C. and 600 A.D. They grew out societies that were, compared to ours, more in tune with rhythms of nature—the cycles of crops and the seasonal rotation—natural rhythms with which we've lost touch.

One has only to turn to the New Testament to see how thoroughly the agricultural context of the society influenced the teachings of Jesus:

> At that time, Jesus took a walk one sabbath day through the cornfields . . .(Mt. 12:1)

> Make a tree sound and its fruit will be sound; make a tree rotten and its fruit will be rotten. For the tree can be told by its fruit. (Mt. 12:33-34)

> He said, 'Imagine a sower going out to sow . . .' (Mt. 13:4)

He put another parable before them, 'The kingdom of heaven may be compared to a man who sowed good seed in his field.' (Mt. 13:24)

I am the true vine,
and my Father is the vinedresser . . . (Jn 15:1)

The list could be multiplied endlessly, including not least the famous admonition that unless a grain of wheat falls in the ground and dies, it cannot live.

In the parables of Buddhism and in the writings of the Upanishads,* too, one finds mythological truths being drawn out of agricultural metaphors. In the Katha Upanishad we read:

Remember how the men of old passed away, and how those of days to come will also pass away: a mortal ripens like corn and like corn is born again.

and

The Tree of Eternity has its roots in heaven above and its branches reach down to earth. It is Brahman, pure Spirit, who in truth is called the Immortal.[6]

Do these sorts of ancient, agricultural images have anything of relevance to say to the world of the strip mall? Or does a new language, a new symbology have to emerge to accommodate new realities? Every age can climb the vertical axis only in terms of what is happening along its own horizontal line, i.e. we cannot be medieval Christians any more than they could have been primitive Christians. The question is, what form can the new geography of the spiritual world take?

In "Church Going," Larkin imagines that someday Christian churches will fall into disuse and ruin as had Stonehenge and the Acropolis. Perhaps scholars will come with their notepads, or the superstitious will come at night to perform half-remembered magic. He sees the old church becoming:

A shape less recognisable each week,

---

[6]*The Upanishads.* Juan Mascaro, tr. London: Penguin Books, 1965.

A purpose more obscure. I wonder who
Will be the last, the very last, to seek
This place for what it was . . .

And yet, he notes, one thing about this place will not pass
away—the inner spiritual need and hunger of the beings who built it
in the first place.

For though I've no idea
What this accoutred frowsty barn is worth,
It pleases me to stand in silence here;

A serious house on serious earth it is,
In whose blent air all our compulsions meet,
Are recognised, and robed as destinies.
And that much never can be obsolete,
Since someone will forever be surprising
A hunger in himself to be more serious,
And gravitating with it to this ground,
Which, he once heard, was proper to grow wise in,
If only that so many dead lie round.[7]

Finding One's Self

The way out of the postmodern world's "geography of nowhere" will not be easy. There is a bit of disingenuousness in the
title of this chapter which is also the subtitle of this book. "Finding
One's Self in the Postmodern World," may look at first glance as if
there were already an answer to the questions we have been asking
so far, or as if there were a technique of some kind for "finding"
oneself in the midst of the current world's confusion. That may
come in time, but first we must deal with the other meaning of "finding oneself" in the postmodern world—that this is, quite simply, the
place where we "find" ourselves, none of us having chosen to be
born and to live in the latter end of the twentieth century. We were,
as the existentialists say, simply "thrown" into this time and place

---

[7]Ibid.

and we have found ourselves washed up on this particular shoal and bank of time and no other.

There is little question that we find ourselves in an age of transition, when ideas, mythologies and social institutions are in flux. Intellectually, it is an age of "deconstruction" and everywhere one turns one sees people casting about for something solid to hang on to. Postmodernism in religion has taken the form of experiments with far eastern Indian and Native American ritual forms, with renewed interest in astrology and witchcraft, with "new" religions that are made up of an eclectic selection of world mythic religions, as though their practitioners had passed through a sort of metaphysical salad bar. The problem in the postmodern world, mythologically speaking, is not that there is no center anymore but that there are too many centers, as devotees of this Way or that Way try to convince others to follow them.

And yet, so little of what goes under the generic heading of "New Age" seems to satisfy for any length of time. We all know people who have "tried" Zen,* transcendental meditation, the Medicine Wheel, aura reading and who knows what all different approaches to the spirit life without finding a permanent home in any of them. First this way, then that are "the" answer, then you meet them a few months later and they've abandoned it altogether and are "into" something else—aromatherapy, for example—with equal zeal.

Why is it so difficult for those of us in the postmodern world to grab hold of anything that we can stay with for any length of time? Or is this sort of "serial monogamy" in mythologies the way things will be from now on?

I think part of the difficulty we have in finding a mythology we can stay with is in the very nature of the postmodern condition as defined by Lyotard. According to Lyotard, it is the loss of belief in the narrative as a mode of knowing that most characterizes life in the postmodern age. It is axiomatic to the modern mind that "mere" stories have nothing to add to the world's storehouse of knowledge. As we tried to show in chapters three and four above, scientific knowledge knocked the pins out from beneath the story as a way of knowing about the world. In the modern lingo, myth, narrative, fiction and fantasy all become synonyms for "falsehood."

Thus, as we noted before, the modern and postmodern mind does not really trust the story to deliver "the goods" in the way of incontrovertible knowledge about life and the universe. We no more than get "into" one religion or another and the scientific mind says, "What are you doing sitting here reading about Rama and the Buddha, chanting and praying? Don't you know that stuff's *irrational*?" And we drop it, float uneasily for a while in the world of late-twentieth century materialism, and then latch onto something else until that skeptical modern voice pops up again.

Of course the pathetic part of the postmodern dilemma is that we have now reached the point when we don't even trust science to deliver us anything like verifiable, objective knowledge. Scientific "facts," we now know, are factual only within the context of a more or less arbitrary and certainly changeable paradigm. Every truth is suddenly relative and we are brutally reminded that the root word of "fact," the Latin *factum* from the verb *facere* (to make), originally meant something made up. Once again, the postmodern mind is at sea.

In spite of the postmodern contention that the narrative mode of knowing is dead, however, we still live in a world of stories. It appears that the human animal will create and live by stories in spite of French philosophies and postmodern ideologies.

We rise in the morning and read newspaper accounts—"stories"—which are nothing but someone else's retelling of events that occurred. In our law courts we hear testimony in which one person's story competes with another's for our belief. Around the office coffeepot, we trade stories in the form of gossip about co-workers. In the evening we watch stories on TV and we tell our spouses the "story" of our day, its heroes and villains, its climaxes and defeats. In psychotherapy we lie or sit and attempt to reconstruct, in the presence of an audience of one, the "story" of how our lives have reached this point.

It goes without saying that all of these stories are merely "as if" propositions, lacking the sort of binary certitude we have come to expect from computers. And, as the postmodernists point out, these texts compete with each other for dominance. Anyone who reads two different newspapers or who has sat through a court trial knows there is no "one" story but that everything is a Rashomon of tales, sometimes mutally contradictory.

And yet, we continue to use stories to gain whatever proximate knowledge and understanding we can have of our condition and of the events in our world. True, narrative does not give us absolute knowledge, but it does give us something. It gives us a specifically human form of knowing that works fairly well when we allow it to.

But it works *differently* from what we have come to call knowledge over the past few hundred years, and as long as we insist that it reveal to us something absolute and objective, we will be disappointed by it.

But it is through the metaphorical way of knowing that the human species has been able to experience a sense of coherence and meaning that today seems so lacking. Even science, in that sense, is a story. The famous equation $E=mc^2$ is nothing but a metaphor which says, essentially, let us explore the universe "as if" energy were equivalent to matter accelerated to the speed of light squared. Only time will tell if this metaphor is "true" or not. In the meantime, it will have to do. Absolute knowledge this is not, but it is human knowledge, limited, fallible—feeling its way forward in the darkness towards increasing light. More importantly, it is the only kind of knowledge we poor forked creatures can have.

And yet it serves us well, when we let it, for what it delivers to us is not so much a content or a "meaning" of life but rather an experience of living.

Narrative knowledge is not abstract or objective. It cannot stand on its own, separate from the teller. To learn how it operates, one must actively participate in the story, via imagination and intuition. Narrative allows us to re*imagine* our lives, not merely re*think* them. In the story we also re*feel* how it is to be human and we re*awaken* the long dormant experience of being alive and connected. In short, the story and its ritual enactments release us to the *participation mystique* which gives us the sense of deep connectedness that we so sorely lack in the modern age. There we experience, not just talk about, meaning in life, and this experience resists contradiction.

The difficulty today, perhaps, is that we've allowed the storytelling and story-listening capacity to so atrophy in us that we distrust its ability to lead us out of the postmodern dilemma. The good news is that this ability did not die but merely lies within us asleep, as a potential waiting to be resurrected. Like the archetypes of Jung, the capacity for story lies dormant until external circumstances call it forth, and now, in the midst of the postmodern condition, it is time to resurrect the story and to relearn the songlines that will carry us through this rather blank postmodern landscape of nowhere.

To do that, however, we must first convince ourselves of the power of the story and even explain, in terms that the conscious mind will understand, exactly how the story functions to supply us with a much needed complement to the modern scientific way of thought.

Over the past fifteen years or so, the work of a curious blend of anthropologists, psychologists, poets and philosophers has been attempting to articulate, in scientific terms, just how mythology, ritual, art and symbolism work to create a sense of wholeness and centeredness in us. *That* these things work to provide human beings with a sense of meaning is fairly clear from the evidence of cultures and individuals who have used them for the past tens of thousands of years. *How* they work is a fascinating area of study that is just opening up, and if we understand better how then we may be more willing to let this realm work in its own distinctive and powerful way.

The Neurophysiology of the Sacred

To begin, let's return to MacLean's model of the triune brain discussed in chapter six. Both as a scientific theory and as a poetic metaphor, it is a perfect model for the "divided self" we often experience for it suggests that the division we feel within ourselves, and even *from* ourselves, is not just a modern or postmodern phenomenon. It is rather something endemic to the human condition, built into the hardwiring of the central nervous system. It is what makes us distinctly human. One does not imagine a salmon feeling divided from its instinctual self, but human beings seem to experience it quite regularly. The development of the highly articulate forebrain had obvious evolutionary advantages for our ancestors, but the price we paid as a species was the divided self that we suffer from so acutely today. The physiological interpretation of the divided self finds its archetypal model in the story of mankind's origins in Genesis, for Adam and Eve ate of the tree of knowledge and became "godlike" in their ability to distinguish such dualities as good and evil, clothed and naked, male and female, God and human. In achieving their new perspective, however, they "fell" from their Edenic *participation mystique* into the division of self from self that we know as the human condition. In the story of mankind's fall from the timeless paradise of Eden into the divided world of time, we may hear the echo of the story of the evolution of the neocortex, a fall from the unreflective world of the apes into the schizoid division of the world of mankind.

Mythology and ritual, those narrative modes of knowing, entered the breach between the ancient reptilian and old mammalian brains and the new, more removed and objective forebrain. For a time, these powerful religious narratives enabled us to live in some harmony with ourselves. Salvation or enlightenment—union with the source of all life—was seen as possible. Even if one mythology displaced another, as Christianity displaced Graeco-Roman mythology in the early centuries of the Christian era, faith in mythology itself as a way of knowing the world and the self did not waver. The realm of the gods was secure, even if the supremacy of any one god or group of gods was precarious. Awareness of their transient nature is buried in many of the myths themselves. The Olympian gods, for example, displaced the Titans, and Zeus himself feared displacement in his turn. His torture of Prometheus—the "forward looking" one who knew the secret of Zeus' overthrow—demonstrates this god's awareness of the transience of his own reign. It is a basic idea in Hinduism, too, that gods come and go but the divine remains eternally. Particular deities may pass away, but there will always be "gods" in some form or another.

Today, however, we doubt the power of any myth or any god to deliver us from our division. We distrust the entire mode of knowing, not just the individual god here or there. The reasons for this are complex, as we tried to show in the chapters on the evolution of modern western consciousness. The breakdown involved both an intentional turning away from mythological ways of thought in favor of rationalism and then, in time, a forgetting of how that older, more "primitive" mode of thought worked. In time, the narrative mode atrophied, and we grew to distrust its abilities. But, just as someone whose broken arm has been in a cast for six weeks can bring the withered, flaccid muscles back to full functioning through therapy, so it is possible to regain the muscle tone of one's atrophied spiritual sense.

The challenge today is to give a plausible, "scientific" explanation for what we have known to be true all along, that myth, ritual, prayer, symbolic activities of all sorts give us a sense of centeredness and wholeness, that they dissolve the logical contradictions of our lives and experience, and thus allow us to continue with the feeling that all is as it should be, the believer's essential insight.

If, as suggested above, the "narrative" forms of knowledge such as myth, ritual, art and symbols form a sort of middle language between the highly verbal neocortex and the deeper, older non-verbal parts of our human brain, then it would be good to explore further the nature of this peculiar communication and how it works and towards what end it is directed.

In an essay published shortly before his death, renowned anthropologist Victor Turner turned to this very question.[8] Advocating a synthesis between cerebral neurology and anthropology, Turner argued that the sources and purposes of what we have called the "narrative" modes of knowing are not just social but may be deeply physiological. That is, ritual behaviors in human beings—including storytelling, ritual dancing, meditation, symbolic activities of all sorts—both arise out of and, in return, act upon physiological processes.

Turner based many of his comments on studies conducted in the 1970's by Eugene D'Aquili, Charles D. Laughlin and others, published in a book entitled *The Spectrum of Ritual: A Biogenetic Structural Analysis.*[9] Briefly, D'Aquili and Laughlin define ritual as structured, repeated behavior involving two or more individuals which results in greater coordination of those individuals towards some social goal. Collective ritual, in other words, is a form of social communication that synchronizes the actions of many individuals into corporate

---

[8]Victor Turner, "Body, Brain and Culture." *Zygon: Journal of Science and Religion,* Sept. 1983. pp. 221-245.

[9]New York: Columbia Univ. Press, 1979.

action of some sort. This is clearly seen in rituals of harvest, for example, wherein the actions of many members of the group must be directed towards the same goal, or the rituals involved in preparation for hunting or war where individuals must be convinced to lay aside their personal interests and well-being for the greater good of the group.

The communication that takes place in ritual thus melds the individual with the group, brings the whole group into synchrony, and gives the entire group a sense of united purpose and identity.

Ritual does not only function on a collective, social basis, however. Ritual also works intrapsychically in such a way that changes occur *within* the individual participant. These changes in neuromotor functions are generally towards greater integration of functions that we normally experience as separate. Rituals, according to D'Aquili and Laughlin, function "as a mechanism for entraining* and transforming the structure of neuromotor subsystems in the developing organism."[10] In other words, participating in the rituals of the tribe over the course of a lifetime actually facilitates the integration of biological and neurological systems that otherwise might be separate. The Songlines of the Australian aborigines, the singing of sacred hymns, chanting a mantra and other ritual behaviors are therefore nothing less than highly refined methods of achieving fuller communication among the various levels of brain we have been discussing.

It is, of course, no news that by participating in ritual an individual feels more "at one" with him/herself and the cosmos. This has been the more or less conscious goal of religions and yogas for centuries, millenia even. The *Svetasvatara Upanishad* describes the technique almost two thousand years ago:

> With upright body, head and neck, lead the mind and its powers into thy heart; and the OM of Brahman will then be thy boat with which to cross the rivers of fear.
>
> And when the body is in silent steadiness, breathe rythmically through the nostrils with a peaceful ebbing and flowing of breath. The chariot of the mind is drawn by wild horses, and those wild horses have to be tamed.[11]

---

[10] Ibid., p. 35.

The goal of this yoga, as given by the *Katha Upanishad*, is "rest in the senses, concentration in the mind, and peace in one's heart."[12]

What is necessary today, however, is to understand these ancient techniques and states of being in terms of the prevailing scientific "myth" of our time. The rational, scientific mind must come to know, in its own way, what, in a sense, has been known all along— that the so-called "narrative" modes of knowing and being perform a valued and even necessary function in the individual and social lives of human beings and cannot be discarded with impunity or simply written off as "superstitions."

According to D'Aquili and Laughlin, the rhythmic chanting, dancing and music that accompany or make up rituals constitute "driving" mechanisms that coordinate various neural systems in the human body. In "The Neurology of Ritual Trance,"[13] Barbara Lex says that such "driving" behaviors facilitate the integration of the human nervous system and thus maintain homeostasis* in the organism. Entering "ritual trance" where the normal distinctions of time, self and place become indistinct is a potential for everyone, for all human beings share the same physiology. According to Lex, this ritual state " . . .arises from manipulation of universal neurophysiological structures of the human body, lies within the potential behavior of all normal human beings, and functions as a homeostatic mechanism for both individuals and groups."[14]

When one participates in the group's rituals, therefore, one achieves a balance both within and without. The collective rhythm of the tribe and the unique rhythm of the individual become one. For the ritual participants this rhythm is also the beat of the universe itself, and thus all three "worlds" are at one:

---

[11]*The Upanishads*, p. 88.

[12]Ibid., p. 60.

[13]in D'Aquili and Laughlin, *op. cit.*

[14]Ibid., p. 118.

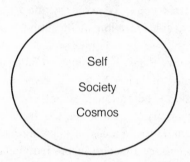

Self

Society

Cosmos

The body's neural rhythms become "entrained" by the rhythms of music, chant, drumming. African tribes, like the Yoruba, may dance for hours or even days until the ritual state is reached. Native American drumming achieves the same end. The old Latin litanies of the pre-Vatican II Catholic church, with their rhythmic interchange between priest and congregation, also served to entrain the rhythm of the individual's neural system to the larger rhythm of the group and, thus, to the realm of the gods.

Similarly, according to Lex, the *absence* of these stimuli can also induce ritual state. For example, in Zen meditation sensory stimuli are purposely removed and the same effect is achieved. In the meditation hall, except for brief periods of chanting sutras, a strict silence is observed. The meditating monks sit motionless for long periods concentrating only on their posture and breathing. After only a brief time, the edges of the self—ego-consciousness—begin to fade away and, eventually, the sense of a self as distinct from other selves and the rest of the world disappears into a feeling of oceanic oneness. The effect is, essentially, the same as that achieved by other means such as drumming, repetitive chanting, etc.

Both kinds of driving behaviors, the hyperexcitement of rhythms or the hypo-excitement of silent meditation, have the same goal—to go beyond the thresholds of "normal" neurophysiological excitation in order to achieve the experience of a united, undivided self. Lex describes this as "a shift from the time-binding, verbal linear mode of thought into a timeless organic gestalt* . . .[This] provides an explanation for subjective reports of temporal distortion and unusual sensation—often inexpressible experiences—presented by persons who have undergone ritual trance."[15]

According to this line of reasoning, meditation, ritual, ceremonial possession, all seem to serve an integrating function in the nervous system between what Lex calls the body's "ergotropic" system, which is concerned with work and activity, and the tropotropic system* which has to do with relaxation. While stimulation of the ergotropic system* results in increased blood pressure, heart rate, increased muscle tone and other characteristics that are manifested most dramatically in the "flight-fight" pattern, stimulation of the tropotropic system reduces most of those characteristics.[16]

These two systems thus form a sort of yin/yang within the body-mind, both necessary for survival, but both at odds with each other, in a sense. Obviously a balance must be maintained between the two systems, and obviously some method of synchronizing these systems would be healthy, but to "tune" them together would involve entering a sort of medial state where we would expect to find a combination of the characteristics of the two states, a state of mind and body that would combine the alertness and focus of the ergotropic system with the relaxation and lack of focus of the tropotropic. This seems to happen in states of ritual trance and meditation. According to Lex, " . . .meditation constitutes a shift in balance in the direction of tropotropic dominance with some degree of ergotropic excitation, combining relaxation of the skeletal muscles with cortical alertness, while in ecstasy both relaxation and mental activity are further heightened."[17]

On the individual level, then, we could say that the ritual actions, whatever they are, provide the practitioners with the necessary stimulation and focus that would bring them to the desired state of integration. The rituals, practiced over time, in effect become stimuli, opening the pathways by which we achieve the balance of our inner neural systems. Making the sign of the cross, chanting a mantra, putting on a vestment, entering a church, are all ways of triggering, as it were, the opening of the neural pathways where our internal systems communicate and find their balance point.

---

[15]Ibid., pp. 125-6.

[16]Ibid., pp. 134-8.

[17]Ibid., p. 138.

D'Aquili and Laughlin attempt to pinpoint the neurological structures responsible for the feelings of wholeness and unity that one experiences in ritual moments. "In the special case of prolonged rhythmic stimuli, one can postulate that the simultaneous strong discharge of both autonomic systems creates a state of stimulation of the median forebrain bundle, generating not only pleasurable sensations but, under proper conditions, a sense of union or oneness with" other members of the species and group.[18]

When a group of people shares these gestures and rituals, they employ a powerful method of attuning the members of the group to one another. The highly standardized gestures of ritual, with their divine sanctions, ideally should defuse inner tensions within the group and reestablish the divinely ordered social hierarchy. The fixed behaviors of the ritual attune, in a literal sense, the rhythms of the individual members of the group to one another. By teaching the rituals to the young, the group socializes them, bringing them by appropriate stages to full adult participation in the life of the tribe. Rites of passage performed at puberty, marriage, death and so on, thus are acknowledgements of new roles in the life of the group and also the means by which one's individual life rhythm becomes attuned to the rhythm of the group.

It is no surprise, therefore, to find religious ritual nearly universally taking the form of chanted poetry, for the rhythmic nature of poetry must correspond to the inner rhythms of the human brain. In a fascinating study recounted in "The Neural Lyre: Poetic Meter, the Brain and Time," Frederick Turner and Ernest Poppel explore the rhythms of metered poetry in many languages and find a near universal rhythm to what they call the metric "pulse" of human poetry and they relate this rhythm to the neurological rhythms of the brain as it processes and integrates information between the two hemispheres of the brain.[19]

"In nearly all cultures," they write, "metered poetry is used in the religious and social (and often economic) rituals, and has the

---

[18]Ibid., pp. 157-8.

[19]Frederick Turner and Ernst Poppel, "The Neural Lyre: Poetic Meter, the Brain and Time," originally published in *Poetry*, August 1983, pp. 277-309. Also reprinted in Frederick Turner, *Natural Classicism*. Charlottesville, Virginia: The Univ. Press of Virginia. 1992. Page references are to original publication.

reputation of containing mysterious wisdom; the learning of major poetic texts is central to the process of education in nearly all literate traditions."[20]

Studying poetry from language groups as various as Chinese, English, Ancient Greek, Uralic, Ndembu (Zambia) and Eipo (New Guinea), Turner and Poppel discovered that the poetic line used in all these languages has a pulse of between two to four seconds, with most lines averaging between 2.5 and 3.5 seconds in duration. The combination, in poetry, of semantic meaning with an acoustical, felt rhythm, combines the functions of the two hemispheres of the brain and synthesizes them. Once again, as in the case of ritual trance above, we are seeing a narrative form functioning to integrate two otherwise fairly independent physiological systems. "If this hypothesis is accurate, meter is, in part, a way of introducing right-brain processes into the left-brain activity of understanding language; and in another sense, it is a way of connecting our much more culture-bound (and perhaps evolutionarily later) linguistic capacities with the relatively more 'hardwired' spatial pattern-recognition faculties we share with the higher mammals."[21]

Rather astonishingly, Turner and Poppel report, the human brain seems to process information in discreet packets which turn out to be about three seconds in duration. That is, a listener will have to pause, as it were, every three seconds in order to absorb information coming in through the ear. "To use a cybernetic* metaphor, we possess an auditory information 'buffer' whose capacity is three seconds' worth of information; at the end of three seconds the 'buffer' is full, and it passes on its entire accumulated stock of information to the higher processing centers."[22] Information arrives and is processed, in other words, in a sort of pulse whose duration is about three seconds, almost the exact interval of length of the pulse of the poetic line found in almost all the languages of the world.

---

[20]Ibid., p. 285.

[21]Ibid., p. 293.

[22]Ibid., p. 296.

The effects of rhythmic chanting of even secular poetry are, not surprisingly, similar to the effects described above of ritual trance and it's worth quoting Poppel and Turner at length here:

> Robert Graves speaks of the shiver and the coldness in the spine, the hair rising on the head and body, as does Emily Dickinson. A profound muscular relaxation yet an intense alertness and concentration is also recorded. The heart feels squeezed and the stomach cramped. There is a tendency toward laughter or tears, or both; the taking of deep breaths; and a slightly intoxicated feeling. . . . At the same time, there is a cataract or avalanche of vigorous thought, in which new connections are made. . . . There is a sense of being on the edge of a precipice of insight—almost a vertigo—and the awareness of entirely new combinations of ideas taking concrete shape, together with feelings of strangeness and even terror. . . . Outside stimuli are often blanked out, so strong is the concentration. The imagery of the poem becomes so intense that it is almost like real sensory experience. . . . There is an intense valorization of the world and of human life, together with a strong sense of the reconciliation of opposites—joy and sorrow, life and death, good and evil, divine and human, reality and illusion, whole and part, comic and tragic, time and timelessness . . . . an experience of time so full of significance that stillness and sweeping motion are the same thing. There is a sense of power combined with effortlessness. . . . There is an awareness of one's own physical nature, of one's birth and death, and of a curious transcendence of them; and, often, a strong feeling of universal and particular love and communal solidarity.[23]

Whew!

We may now take a deep breath and return to anthropologist Victor Turner's article, "Body, Brain and Culture," with which we started this discussion. Through most of his career, Turner was a structuralist,* which is to say, like most anthropologists he had been trained to regard human institutions and social patterns as more or less arbitrarily arrived at conventions, learned behaviors, not behaviors based on deep neurological structures of the human brain. MacLean's work on the tripartite human brain, however, moved Turner to question these assumptions and to consider whether ritual

---

[23]Ibid., pp. 299-300.

form was in fact related to biological function and whether, in fact, it served some sort of role in synthesizing the higher mental functions with the genetic information encoded in the deeper centers of the brain.

If so, then ritual becomes, as we have suggested above, a means of carrying on communication between the various parts of the brain, a common language, largely non-verbal, by which the forward looking neocortex can "talk" with the conservative reptilian and old mammalian brains. The ritual, and what is experienced in the ritual trance, is directed towards integration, synthesis and wholeness, providing, as it were, a middle ground in which new information from the environment may be checked on an ongoing basis with old, tested wisdom stored deep in the brain. In the "liminal"* or threshold state of ritual trance—or, for that matter, poetic or aesthetic rapture—one enters into an intermediate zone between normal consciousness and deep sleep where, as in dreams, transformations take place.

If one denies oneself this sort of ritual activity, as we could say the modern world has done in its denegration of ritual forms and the "mere" stories that give rise to them, then one runs the risk of ending up in a state of fragmentation, alienation, anxiety, fear, dread, despair, and all the other states of being into which the contemporary world has fallen. We have, in effect, cut ourselves off from one of the most potent neurophysiological survival mechanisms the human species possesses, what, up until fairly recent times, has been called the realm of the gods.

"Just make noise!"

The point of this long excursion into neurobiology is not only that one discards the realm of the gods at great risk, but also that the doorway back into that realm is never far away. The forms may change from culture to culture and age to age, gods may come and gods may go, but beneath the specific cultural manifestations of world religions and the plethora of bewildering rituals there are some constants. Those constants might best be understood, at this point anyway, as the neurobiological structures of the human organism it-

self, the goal of which is to maintain some sort of homeostasis both
within the organism and between the organism and the outside world.

The particular form is less relevant than that there *be* a form in
which the individual and the culture finds regular access to that liminal state of mind where all of life's oppositions may be reconciled.
This might best be illustrated by a personal anecdote.

Some years ago, I made a weekend retreat at a Zen temple. It
was my first real experience with Zen other than reading and a brief
introduction to Zen breathing and postures given to me by a Catholic
priest who had been experimenting with Oriental meditation techniques in the late 1960's.

When I arrived at the temple, I was somewhat unnerved by the
shaved heads, the strange robes, the incense and all the paraphernalia
of the Buddha hall and the monks. Part of the reason I had found
myself attracted to Zen was its insistence on simplicity and getting
away from icons to point at the heart of things, so I was surprised by
the ornateness of everything. Somewhat cowed, I asked the priest for
some guidance on proper behavior at the temple, but he simply said,
"Just watch and do."

When I pressed him further, he said we would be sitting in
zazen for some time and then we would chant briefly between ses-
sions.

"Do you have the words for the chants?" I asked. I had seen
sheets in another temple with phonetic transcriptions of the sutras,
but the priest rather brusquely said, "No sheets. You just make
noise" and he walked away in disgust at my obtuseness.

And so I just made noise. As the monks in the hall chanted the
ancient sutras, I made gutteral monosyllabic sounds in the same
rhythm. And it worked.

Over the years since then, I have heard more than one Zen
priest admit that he himself did not know the exact meaning of the
words of the sutras he chanted. Written in archaic Japanese or Ko-
rean, chanting them would be the equivalent of our chanting in An-
glo-Saxon or of singing the Latin hymns I had learned by rote in my
Catholic boyhood. Some words would be familiar, certain formulaic
phrases would repeat frequently, but in the final analysis it was not
the *meaning* of the words that mattered, for the words were only an

excuse to engage in the rhythmic chanting which, regardless of the semantic content of the particular hymn or sutra, would serve as a "drive behavior"* to help us achieve the sense of balance, integration and unity that is the point of ritual in the first place.

A few years ago, I attended the funeral of a Roman Catholic monsignor who had once been president of the college where I teach. It was a solemn high mass, officiated by the bishop and concelebrated by nearly eighty priests of all ages. In view of the monsignor's age, the English liturgy was interspersed with Latin hymns. These Latin hymns had not been sung, as a rule, since the mid-1960's when the liturgical reforms of Vatican II disposed of the old Latin mass. Nonetheless, I noticed an amazing thing happen during the singing of the Latin hymns. After a lapse of over twenty years, the words and melodies were still on—or perhaps "in"—my lips. I could actually sing them from memory, for the most part. As I looked around the congregation I noticed that others who were my age or older were also singing the Latin hymns largely from memory while they were forced to look on the page for the words of the hymns in English.

Perhaps *because* they were in a foreign language—a dead and ancient one at that—they remained buried in the long-term memory, revived in the ritual ambience of the high mass in which we had learned them. I found the experience quite moving, and after the mass I discussed this phenomenon with other older Catholics and all of them seemed equally surprised at how easily the unpracticed hymns came back, and several remarked at how "meaningful" the hymns were, more so even than the modern hymns in English whose words we could understand. I would guess that the experience is similar for Jews who chant or sing in a Hebrew tongue that they might not fully understand.

Perhaps, in terms of the intended effect of ritual, it is even better to sing in a language we don't understand because then the rather left-brained, analytical content of most hymns (which in Christian churches often amount to theological tracts *about* God rather than prayers *to* him) actually get in the way.

As the Zen priest said, maybe the point is to "just make noise."

But is it really? After all this discussion of neurobiology, are we to conclude that all the great religious and mythological traditions of the world are nothing more than drive behaviors to pull off some sort of neurological sleight-of-hand whereby firing nerve endings from competing hemispheres and levels of the brain may communicate with each other? In that case, couldn't the effect be achieved more easily via drugs or therapy? And if ritual form and mythological narratives are nothing more than drive behaviors, then is the particular form of the ritual irrelevant? Is it all, after all, "just noise"?

These are questions to which answers must be found if we are ever to get out of the quagmire of relativism into which we've fallen in the postmodern world and to answer them, we may have to enter an unknown territory that we, as a species, have not gone into before.

CHAPTER 8

*Terra Incognita**

AT A CLIMACTIC MOMENT EARLY IN JAMES JOYCE'S *A PORTRAIT of the Artist as a Young Man*, Mrs. Riordan, Stephen's "Dante," attempts to end an argument over religion and politics by shrieking out, "God and religion before everything! . . . God and religion before the world!"

Her opponent, however, is not easily cowed.

"Mr. Casey raised his clenched fist and brought it down on the table with a crash.

—Very well, then, he shouted hoarsely, if it comes to that, no God for Ireland! . . . We have had too much God in Ireland. Away with God!"[1]

In surveying the news from nowhere that we find in today's newspapers and TV news programs, it is tempting to shout, with Mr. Casey, "We have had too much of God in this world. Away with God, away with all the gods!"

On some days, it is an attractive proposition. A quick survey of the world's hot spots reveals that at the heart of many of the disputes over which human beings are willing to kill themselves are religious differences which, to outsiders, seem inconsequential.

To cite just a few examples will suffice. In sixteenth-century India, a Mughal built a Moslem mosque over the site of an earlier temple to Rama. In 1992, a dispute over the Babri Masjid mosque in the ancient Hindu holy city of Ayodhya led to years of riots in which many people were killed. Analysts see the unrest as a Hindu re-

---

[1] James Joyce, *A Portrait of the Artist as a Young Man*. New York: The Viking Press, 1964. p. 39.

sponse to rising Muslim fundamentalism and to the increasing "westernization" of India.

In the Middle East, for at least a thousand years now, Christians, Muslims and Jews have been at each other's throats in spite of the fact that these three religions have much in common. The latest rounds of wars and riots may be seen as continuations of ancient medieval rivalries that have never been resolved.

In the Balkans, Roman Catholic Serbs, Orthodox Christian Croatians and ethnic Muslims commit such atrocities as "ethnic cleansing" and mass rape on each other.

In Northern Ireland, for the past twenty years, Catholic Christians have been blowing up Protestant Christians and vice versa in a continuation of a conflict that has been raging at least since the time of Richard II.

While all these conflicts have economic, racial and social causes, the religious differences at least serve as a sort of shorthand for dividing up sides. We might even say that far from bringing people together, religion does little but drive them apart.

Closer to home, religion is fueling battles in American suburbs over school curriculum. In 1992, the Michigan Department of Education developed a comprehensive plan for teaching health awareness which included a section on relaxation in which students were to be taught to use controlled breathing to reduce stress. The plan came under bitter attack from Christian fundamentalists who claimed that the breathing exercises were actually a form of Oriental meditation and "therefore" a form of mind control, Satan worship and a threat to Christian values. The breathing exercises—and a section on birth control methods—were dropped from the curriculum. In Georgia, meanwhile, yoga classes were suspended in a small town where Christians claimed yoga was "a heathen activity akin to devil worship." In California and elsewhere, movements have been mounted to ban books that have been deemed irreligious from schools.

Political leaders, too, have wielded the sword of religion to divide, if not (yet) to conquer America. At the 1992 Republican National Convention, would-be presidential candidates Pat Robertson and Patrick Buchanan delivered chilling sermons, in the name of "family values," against homosexuals, intellectuals, liberals and others who did not fit their narrow definition of "moral." Patrick Buchanan even declared that "There is a religious war for the soul of America" going on and George Bush proclaimed that the three letters missing from the Republican platform were "G-O-D." It was clear that this God was white, Christian and male.

On the political left, meanwhile, the forces of "political correctness" have arrayed themselves against the discussion of religious and spiritual values and thus have split college campuses, school systems and political parties in the name of an ill-defined "secular humanism" which frightens many God-fearing Christians.

Outside the mainstream of politics and social movements, we find religion again being a cause of destruction and separation. Fringe religious groups like David Koresh's Branch Davidian sect in Waco, Texas, proclaiming themselves God's chosen people, arm themselves with Bibles and modern weapons for violent, self-fulfilling confrontations that will mark the end of days.

Sometimes the gods seem to do more harm than good. If they more often seem to bring the sword than the means of peace, then wouldn't it be better to do away with them altogether? Wouldn't the human race benefit by ridding itself of these irrational deities who frequently lead it on to the paths of destruction?

The brief answer, of course, is no, for it has already been tried and it hasn't worked. A large part of the project of modernism, as we have seen, was an attempt to do away with the gods and to establish human knowledge, society and life on a purely rational basis. From the separation of church and state in the United States Constitution through the rational *machines a habiter* of Le Corbusier, to the current debates over banning prayer in schools, we in the west have been trying to separate the sacred and the profane for several centuries. The noble goal of this was to establish human life on a purely logical basis and, ultimately, to bring us to a rational Utopia. After a few hundred years of this, however, can we say that things are really any better in the world? Has the triumph of rationalism really reduced, overall, the store of human misery, or has it simply shifted that misery around? True, we have had impressive successes that no one would want to see reversed. The modern world has conquered diseases, greatly reduced infant mortality and extended the life span.

Similarly, many social evils—e.g. slavery—have largely been done away with, and in most parts of the world there seems to be a growing recognition that the rule of law is preferable to the rule of the iron fist or the anarchic mob. But at the same time, as we're only too aware, the "triumph of rationalism" has brought about new and more efficient means of mass slaughter, an overburdening of the earth's ecosystems, much moral confusion and new problems which are often the result of the very solutions rationalism tried to apply to the world's ills.

The fact is, of course, that rationalism alone will never satisfy us. It never has, for, in spite of all, there is, in Huston Smith's phrase, a sort of "spiritual tropism" in the human animal which makes us, as individuals and as a species, turn towards the world of the gods the way that certain flowers turn towards and follow the sun. It's in the genetic code. Just as it is in the nature of seeds to send their roots down into the earth and their shoots up to the sun, so, too, human beings must turn their souls upwards and inwards towards the gods. Sometimes these gods, being the gods of humankind, lead us into the all-too-human arts of war, and sometimes they lead us into the ways of peace, but we must seek them out, by various names, in all times and places because we are the sort of creatures that we are. Some faith in something seems inevitable, even necessary, for us to function.

The problem now, however, is that we have lost faith in faith, and so the challenge before us is not somehow to "unlearn" what we have discovered from three hundred years of science and simply embrace old faiths again. The real challenge is once again to find the will to believe and then to undertake the task of integrating what we *know* about life on earth with metaphors (symbols) that will be embracing enough to allow us to live and be in a state of integration with ourselves, our society and our world. Faith, however, is not easy in the postmodern world, as if it was ever easy in *any* world. Those who are in thrall to their gods—as the fundamentalists seem to be—reject the knowledge of science, and those who embrace science have difficulty with faith because they have become too conscious of faith as "mere" faith to give themselves fully to it. When T. E. Huxley coined the term "agnostic" in the last century, he was speaking for the modern scientific mind in refusing to believe anything that could not be demonstrated by proofs acceptable to reason. This was a precarious enough position in the late 1800's, but the current dilemma is even worse for the postmodern mind knows now that even the proofs of reason are, deep down, unreliable and so we are burdened with the knowledge that any faith we have is "merely" a metaphor standing for something else, and in a world where cultures are colliding with each other with greater frequency and intensity, we have come to believe that no one metaphor or system seems to hold any more (or less) of the truth than any other and so we flounder in relativism.

Thomas Carlyle, the first of the great Victorian sages, called the root of this problem "self-consciousness," by which he meant the inability of modern people to let go of that rational, critical, analytical side of the self and simply *live* spontaneously and unreflectively as, we suppose, our ancestors did. We can no longer enter—because we no longer trust—the state of soul that anthropologists have dubbed *participation mystique.* In our time, we have labelled Carlyle's "self-consciousness" the "postmodern condition," a sadly too-sophisticated realization of the metaphor *as* metaphor which makes full participation in it virtually impossible. This is strange new territory for human consciousness, a consequence of our "fall" from the undivided Eden of *participation mystique* into the intellectual confusion of competing and interchangeable paradigms.

Now, it is a fairly evolved and complex consciousness which recognizes metaphors as such, and yet, perhaps thanks to our modern education, this is where surprisingly large numbers of people are at today. When we speak of searching for a spiritual "center" for postmodern life, or when we invoke a "heaven up there" or speak of an "inner" journey of the "soul," we are painfully aware that the referents of these metaphors are not "out there" in any objective sense. We are self-consciously aware that we are living in a mental world of "as if" constructions, life in the subjunctive mood, where every statement about "life" or "truth" or "God" must be put in quotation marks to indicate that you understand the irony of even using such words in these intellectually troubled times.

This distinctly postmodern consciousness is not something biologically inherited like the color of one's hair, but we could nonetheless make a case for its being a step onward in the gradual evolution of human consciousness which had its physiological beginning in the evolution of the forebrain some millions of years ago. The initial split between the ancient reptilian-old mammalian brains, which function more or less on the level of *participation mystique*, and the modern neocortex (see Chapter Seven) was not that wide. One could see its evolution, however, as the narrow end of a wedge that, over the past several millennia, has driven itself deeper until the gap between the unconscious self and the too-conscious self seems, to many, to be unbridgeable.

But the situation is not as desperate as it seems for the means exist for bridging this ancient gap. They lie dormant in each of us in the form of those potentials we discussed in the last chapter. In the neurophysiological "hardwiring" of the human nervous system, the mechanisms for closing the postmodern wound are already in place. And we know that these are triggered by metaphors, in one form or another. Mythological narratives, ritual chants, ritual dance—these "drive" behaviors work to heal the divided self, *not* because there is any propositional "truth" in them but simply because they work to bring our out-of-phase internal systems into synchrony, and, when practiced with a group, to bring our individual selves into synchrony with the rhythms of our tribe and ultimately of the cosmos itself.

The particular shape of the metaphor is, therefore, fairly irrelevant. God, Allah, Vishnu, Boomba, Quetzalcoatl, Kali, Parvati, the Blessed Virgin—any of the thousands of masks that the divine wears all function well to bring the self into union with itself and the world around it. This is not a new idea. It was expressed most eloquently in the *Baghavad Gita* when Vishnu-Krishna arose and manifested himself in his ten thousand guises and called himself by his ten thousands names.

The Blessed Lord spoke:
Behold, son of Prtha, my forms,
A hundredfold, rather a thousandfold.
Various, divine,
And of various colors and shapes.

. . . .
Behold now the entire universe
With everything moving and not moving,
Here standing together in My Body.

And so Arjuna sees the many mouths, eyes, ornaments and masks of
God facing in all directions at once. He sees there:

. . . the entire universe, standing as one,
Divided in many ways, . . .
In the body of the God of Gods

and he bows his head in a reverent gesture as he acknowledges the
divine power, saying

I see Thee everywhere, infinite in form;
Not the end, nor the middle, nor yet the beginning of Thee
I see, O Lord of All, whose Form is the Universe.[2]

As the composers of the *Gita* knew, each of the many masks of
God is a metaphor for the immense power that may be fully experienced but only inadequately expressed by the myriad names of God.
All of these names are tried and true metaphors and they all have
worked well in their time and place. Any one will do the work of
all. But it is essential that human beings choose *some* name, that
there be *some* metaphor, or else the integration mechanisms won't
work. Just as the lever needs a fulcrum, so the mind needs a spiritual metaphor to enable it to do its work of integration. By abandoning the metaphoric mode, or declaring it dead, the postmodern
mind jettisoned the most valuable piece of equipment it has for
healing itself.

To rediscover and reexperience the power of the metaphor, even
to develop new ones heretofore unseen, is the gauntlet thrown down
before us, and in order to see our way, we need to understand two
apparently contradictory tendencies in the contemporary world that
form a paradox at the heart of the postmodern dilemma. In doing
this, we must keep in mind that a paradox is only an *apparent* contradiction, not a real one.

---

[2]*The Baghavad Gita,* Winthrop Sargent, tr. Albany: State Univ. of New York, 1984. pp.
457-468.

The Paradox of the Postmodern World

When we look at the postmodern world we live in, we see that on the one hand there seems to be increasing uniformity in lifestyles, economy and knowledge in the global community while on the other hand there is increasing fragmentation and diversity.

On the level of technology, for example, most of the world has adopted the metric system of measurement, and the scientific model has made medicine, architecture and engineering similar virtually everywhere. International marketing has made it possible to see the same corporate logos in virtually any country of the world. Waking up in a Tokyo hotel room one may look out the window and see a Canada Dry truck parked in the lot below and a McDonald's restaurant across the street. In their own strange way, Coca-Cola, Sony and Mercedes are making the world one.

Standardizataion of computer components, compact disks and cassette tapes adds to the world's homogenization. Television, too, is essentially the same in Japan, the United States, South America or Europe. Even if the programming and language differ from continent to continent, TV is still TV—a grammar of fast cuts and smiling faces, a strange window on the world that obliterates traditional distinctions between here and there, now and then. Similarly, airports in Detroit, Paris, Hong Kong or Bangladesh must be essentially the same. Planes couldn't land if each nation had its own "kind" of airport the way it has its own kind of cuisine. An automobile is an automobile whether on the streets of Caracas, Venezuela or Dallas, Texas, and it will manifest its own "auto-logic" no matter which culture it appears in. Likewise, one finds western-style business suits in Riyadh, Genoa and Sri Lanka. Thanks to electronic communications and computer networks, the global economy reverberates as one nearly twenty-four hours a day as the Nikkei Index, the NASDAQ and the Dow-Jones send nearly instantaneous vibrations between the Ginza, Wall Street and Bond Street.

At the same time that the world is becoming more and more unified, however, there has been a countermovement, manifested in an upsurge of fundamentalism not only in this country but, more spectacularly, in the Islamic world where, in reaction to decades of "westernization," fundamentalists are asserting their local traditions and laws in ways that are frankly baffling to outsiders. From classroom book bannings in the American Midwest to the enforcement of the *chador* in Teheran, indigenous peoples are insisting on their right to resist the headlong plunge into modernism and postmodernism.

This is a strange new world we live in, a real *terra incognita*, full of dragons and as-yet-unknown terrors. It is a world where Buddhist monks write sutras on mini-computers, where middle class white businessmen take to the woods on weekends to chant and drum in Native American sweat lodges, where the Dalai Lama becomes a sort of pop icon and appears on the cover of *People* magazine along with movie stars and diet gurus, where cultures are colliding against each other at a pace and to a degree that makes the head swim. There seems to be no order beneath the chaos.

And yet, I think, a pattern is discernible. It is a pattern that should be a cause for hope rather than despair, one that leads forward into the future rather than hearkening back to an irretrievable past, for the paradox of postmodern life is that *both* the new internationalism and the new regionalism are the stirrings of a new world and worldview which is, even now, coming into existence.

One hundred years ago, Matthew Arnold, in his "Stanzas from the Grand Chartreuse," wrote of feeling that he was:

> Wandering between two worlds, one dead,
> The other powerless to be born.

One hundred years later, as we approach the end of the twentieth century of the Christian era, we may be able to say that the power which was lacking to midwife the new world in Arnold's time has at last been found and it may be that the "problem" of postmodernism will actually turn out to be its own best solution.

"Once Upon a Time" : A New Beginning

I once had a history professor who cautioned us never to underestimate the historical importance of the time we were living in. From the perspective of five hundred years from now, he said, the twentieth century will be seen as an age of transition equal in importance to the future of the world as the Renaissance was to the future of Europe. It was one of those passing comments that professors make on their way to somewhere else, but the idea stuck with me long after the dates and names from the particular course had disappeared from my memory.

Someone living in Florence in the early fourteenth century would have had no way of knowing the glories of the Italian Renaissance that were to come. He or she would have no way of predicting the emergence of artists like Leonardo or Michelangelo, or of the intellectual consequences of the rebirth of learning that would lead through the invention of the printing press to the Reformation and the beginning of the scientific revolution. For Florentines in 1300, the future was, no doubt, a mirror as dark and obscure as it is for us.

And yet, to someone who was sensitive to the currents of the age, there must have been a feeling that something new was coming to life. In the first stirrings of Dante's Sweet New Style, there must have been a sense of a new world about to be born, bringing with it a lightening and infusion of energy, a feeling that the heaviness of the old medieval ways of thought were falling away even though the shape of what was to come was not yet known.

The twentieth century, too, has been an age of immense transition, and, as in all such ages, there has been much upheaval and destruction (not to mention deconstruction). The doomsayers of our era have seen this as an end, a terminal state of confusion and fragmentation from which there can be no recovery, a permanent state of postmodernism. They speak as though no progress has been made since Arnold found himself lost between two worlds. And yet, progress has been made, at least in the areas we have been focusing on in this book.

In our more optimistic moments, it may even be possible to sense the birth throes of a new age that is coming on. That the transition to this new age is just beginning and that it might take a few hundred years or so to come to fruition should not bother us particularly any more than it would have bothered our imaginary Florentines not to know about the High Renaissance ahead.

Perhaps we are now far enough into the postmodern consciousness to say at least this: the upheavals we are experiencing in politics, culture and religion are nothing less than the dissolution of what has been, for two thousand years or more, a fairly coherent worldview, but they are not the *end* of anything at all. The sense of dissolution, fragmentation and disintegration that has been so well documented by twentieth century artists is real, but it is merely a way station on a much longer journey. In fact, from our current perspective we could even say that the destruction of the old way was necessary, just as it is necessary to destroy a tree in order to create a piano. Destruction of the old and creation of the new fit into one another like hand in glove, like yin and yang. Oracles and worldviews come and go like the body's constant sloughing off of old cells and the regeneration of new ones. One simply has to accept that beneath the apparent change of form something constant remains and that is what seems difficult to do right now.

Today, in a world that seems so overwhelmed by competing stories that we experience nothing but confusion, we must remember that underneath the apparent chaos there is really only one human story. Just as the famous photograph of the planet Earth taken from the Apollo spacecraft in 1968 gave us a view of a unified Earth in which our national and tribal boundaries were invisible and irrelevant, so, too, the work of twentieth century ethologists* and anthropologists has showed us that beneath the seemingly infinite diversity of human mythologies, rituals and social organizations, there is, in the end only one human story. The work of researchers like Adolf Bastian, James Frazier, Mircea Eliade, and Robin Fox, of writers like Joseph Campbell, Huston Smith, Marija Gimbutas and the host of others who are today exploring the areas where human cultures agree, all point to an enduring deep form of human wisdom embodied in the dazzling array of metaphors and myths that make up the body of the world's mythology.

And today, I believe, a new story is emerging, a meta-narrative that may help us, as the Apollo photograph helped us, to see that beneath the world of confusion there is an eternal form. As yet, the story is just beginning. We have barely said "Once upon a time," but the shape of what's to come can at least be hinted at, and even though we cannot expect a "happily ever after" ending, the end outcome should be a greater conscious awareness of the dynamics that drive us as individuals and as a species and that should move us beyond mere "tolerance" of one another to a sort of "deep ecumenism" where the many Songlines of the human race will blend together into the single story of humankind. We may then, at last, learn to celebrate our differences instead of killing ourselves over them.

Who will lead us into this new story? Those who have always led us—the dreamers, the poets and the visionaries of all stripes. They will be all those out on the edges right now, away from the mainstream, who are breaking the old forms, revitalizing old religions, crossing boundaries and thinking what had previously been called the unthinkable. In that sense, all the postmodern experimentation, the crossing of genre lines, the merging of myths are really not about disintegration but form a sort of rich soup of creativity out of which the new forms of the ancient songlines will arise to make a geography of somewhere out of the nowhere in which we currently live.

The new directions will grow out of old knowledge. If the modern malaise is a loss of what traditionally had been called "spirit," then we must first find ways for individuals to gain their souls back. Only then can we create a collective soul which might help to redeem the postmodern world's geography of nowhere. So, to begin, it will be an individual quest. Each of us must accept the responsibility to "lead the mind with all its powers into the heart"[3] and there to experience the eternal within us. After that, we must find the new forms to express it.

It is impossible to predict what specific shapes these new forms of ancient truths will take. Any attempt to prognosticate that way is probably doomed to failure. But anyone who undertakes an essay like this one should be prepared at least to point out a few directions where the new forms may be found.

Clearly new metaphors are needed that will integrate our modern knowledge of the universe with the ancient needs for balance and wholeness that reside in the deepest parts of our central nervous system. This form will have to be some kind of "narrative," for, as we saw in Chapter Seven, the narrative forms of story, dance, music and

---

[3]*The Upanishads.* Juan Mascaro, tr., New York: Penguin, 1965, p. 88.

art, have the unique power to give us the experience of unity that we so sorely lack today. It is the nature of human knowledge to narratize, to live by a series of "as if" propositions, to understand through comparison, analogy and participation, and we must learn our way back to these modes of knowing.

Just as, in the tenth millennium B.C. or so, the ancient hunting mythologies gave way to the grain myths, so today we need to find appropriate forms by which to express our true relationships to ourselves, the earth and those with whom we live.

The new narrative, as it emerges, must include science, though it need not be "scientific." What we have learned from science about the origin of the universe and the origin of the human race must somehow be accounted for or we will continue to live in the rather schizoid way that separates science from mythology. To live in continued separation will only exacerbate the problem. Clearly the world's mythmakers must come to grips with things like the Big Bang Theory and Evolution and realize that the knowledge we have gained from science is not inimical to a sacred understanding of the origin of the Earth. In fact, properly understood, the findings of science can lead us to the new metaphors we will need to rejoin ourselves, our society and our world.

To begin with, we must find a new dominant metaphor for our relationship to nature. One thing that we should have learned by now from our science is that whatever else we are, we are *not* masters of this planet we live on. If anything, we are guests on the planet, living on the kindness of the oxygen producing plants and the food we eat. Our *hybris* must give way to humility. One way we in the west are attempting to do this is through the incorporation of other mythic traditions like the Native American and Oriental traditions where the human species' relationship to the rest of creation has always been one of a dependent to a parent rather than a master to a slave. Out of the western world, there is even a new sort of "myth" arising in the form of Lovelock's Gaia Hypothesis which has gained a currency astonishing for a scientific theory, to the extent that it has entered the vocabulary of people who have never otherwise heard of either Lovelock or the ancient Earth goddess after whom his hypothesis takes its name.

Something of a scientific myth, the Gaia Hypothesis arose out of English chemist J. E. Lovelock's involvement in a study to find life on Mars. In these studies the question "What is life?" had to be answered so that the Mars probe would recognize it if it found it. Through this intriguing question, Lovelock developed the idea that "the earth's biosphere, atmosphere, oceans and soil constitute a feedback or cybernetic system which results in an optimal physical and chemical environment and in the characteristics of living things."[4]

According to Lovelock's hypothesis, the earth itself has a sort of global intelligence which maintains the narrow window of conditions necessary for life as we know it to exist on the planet. The stability of the ratios of gases in the atmosphere over the millions of years' history of the planet is astonishing, says Lovelock. Oxygen breathing animals, including humans, may have evolved, suggests the Gaia hypothesis, in order to help consume this gas that otherwise is poisonous to the carbon-dioxide breathing plants. In return the plants give us oxygen which they don't need in order to create for themselves the necessary CO_2.

Accepting this idea as a working hypothesis, we find that the ancient wisdom of the myths accords with the views of modern science. We are children of a great and wise mother, but, being prodigal, we have strayed from the paths she laid out for us and are paying the price now. This new scientific metaphor also accords with what the poets have told us. For if we believe that we evolved along with the rest of the creatures on the Earth and so are not a special creation, separate in status, then we can, with Wordsworth, marvel with mind and soul at:

> How exquisitely the individual Mind
> . . . to the external World
> is fitted—and how exquisitely, too . . .
> the external World is fitted to the Mind.[5]

But clearly any new mythology must also account for other "new realities." In the past, for example, given the nature of life on

---

[4]Rene Dubos, *Celebrations of Life*. New York: McGraw Hill, 1981, p. 190.

[5]"Prospectus to *The Excursion*" in *Romantic Poetry and Prose*, Harold Bloom and Lionel Trilling, eds. New York: Oxford Univ. Press, 1973. p. 142.

earth, it was necessary for humans to reproduce in great numbers in order for the species to provide enough replacements for the parents who would die. Because of reductions in infant mortality and improvements in public health worldwide, however, unlimited reproduction of the sort practiced by humans in the past has ceased to be a survival strategy and now actually is a threat. Ancient drives towards massive numbers of offspring must be rechannelled somehow. Any new myth must somehow "narratize" this scientific reality.

In the same way, our notion of subduing the earth must give way to an understanding that we must work in accord with the ways of the earth, that we are its servants or stewards and not the other way around.

Just as the modern mythmakers must develop new metaphors for our relationship to the earth, so, too, must we develop new metaphors for our relationships to one another. The dominant metaphor for social relationships in the western world for at least the past hundred years or so has been competition. Mis-reading Darwin, Social Darwinists like Herbert Spencer saw nature "red in tooth and claw" and assumed that human social organization had to be the same. Using this logic, many an unethical capitalist has justified crushing his opposition and despoiling the earth. Any new myth should properly incorporate what Darwin really said, that each species, in the struggle to survive, finds a niche in the ecosystem. Evolution does not necessarily favor the strongest. A barracuda is obviously "stronger" than a sponge, but each survives and thrives in its own way. Perhaps a model of human society should be built on a metaphor of cooperation rather than competition. As in symbiosis, an argument for compassion and cooperation can be argued from biological evidence as easily as *laissez faire* capitalism.

Similarly, human aggression, once a survival mechanism that was glorified in myth and legend, must be relearned. The ancient aggressive mechanisms, that we now know are buried deep in the nervous system, won't just go away if we think "happy thoughts" or become vegetarians. We must learn how to acknowledge the presence of the tendency, but to find new non-destructive ways of applying it. In the old days, when hostile tribes would gang up and go over the nearest hill and beat up on the next available tribe with clubs or spears, aggression was a plausible survival strategy. Today that natural tendency has led us to the development of nuclear weapons which could destroy life on Earth. Like reproducing in large numbers, human aggression may have become a survival strategy which now works *against* survival. This, too, must find its way into the new human story.

From all of this, it should be obvious that it is in the interests of artists and storytellers and religious mystics today to study modern science, not to become scientists but to find in science a body of metaphors that can be fit into the new emerging narrative.

If we need new metaphors for our relationship to the earth and to our fellow beings, we in the *post*-postmodern world will also need a new metaphorical understanding of our relationship to ourselves. Clearly we know too much today about biological drives and unconscious processes to ever again define human beings as merely "rational animals." The body of evidence indicates that reason and logic are afterthoughts, late developments of human consciousness that may even sit on top of a deeper consciousness like snow atop a mountain. If a new mythology is to emerge, we must acknowledge the limits of our human logic and of human logic's greatest invention, science. In our life as we experience it, we are not presented with such binomial oppositions as love/hate, loyalty/treachery, good/evil. Logic can help us sort things out, but ultimately our decisions must come from other sources. We need to relearn to act from our deeper levels, to see feelingly and re-establish trust between the logical, analytic side of our selves and the creative, intuitive side. The studies of Jung and other depth psychologists provide us with a beginning, as does the ancient wisdom of the myths of primal peoples the world over.

Finally, we need to discover a new metaphor for understanding the relationship of all of the above to the universe as a whole, something akin to the Renaissance's Great Chain of Being. We must again realize with humility that we are not alone, isolated, exiled on a planet in the middle of a vast universe of emptiness, but that we are an intimate, integrated part of a vast process we don't even begin to comprehend.

This is a tall order, and in our present state of mind and culture it is difficult to rouse the energy required to scale the heights but, if the past is any guide, we will find the new metaphors we need in the place they've always been, in that much-degraded realm that we used to call the spirit or soul which is as deep within us as it was in our ancestors for millions of years.

The way to this deeper self is well-known, but it resists talking about. We do know this about it, however:

> The way that can be spoken of
> Is not the constant way;
> The name that can be named
> Is not the constant name.
> The nameless is the beginning of heaven and earth.[6]

It also resists intellectualization:

> Not through much learning is the Atman reached, not
> through the intellect and sacred teaching.[7]

So what is the path? What is the way? Is there only one or are there many? Can we even talk about it?

Of course, we can talk about it, but language alone is not enough. Words must be the bridges to experience, mere transitions, forgotten once the goal is reached. Ultimately, we must *live* our way back into the unity we have lost in the postmodern world. We must dance, sing and chant, paint, and *feel* our way, just as our ancestors did before us.

The world today seems utterly different than the world which preceded us, but how much of that difference is real and how much of it has been erected by Maya, the god of illusion? The questions asked at the beginning of the Kena Upanishad almost 3,000 years ago remain the same questions we must ask today and answer in our own terms:

> Who sends the mind to wander afar? Who first drives life to start on its journey? Who impels us to utter these words? Who is the Spirit behind the eye and the ear?[8]

---

[6] Lao Tzu, *Tao te Ching*, D. C. Lau, tr. New York: Penguin, 1963.

[7] *The Upanishads*, Juan Mascaro, tr. New York: Penguin, 1965, p. 60. The Atman is the Hindu concept of the great Self which is within each of us and is the manifestation of the universal energy of Brahman in each individual.

It is the same question asked by the disciples of Jesus: "How then shall we live?"

If we pursue these ancient questions, we should arrive at answers that, in essence, will speak to us in our own language the ancient message that lay underneath the myths that came before.

As Jesus said, the whole secret is "Love one another as I have loved you."

As Confucius said, "Do unto others as you would have them do unto you."

As the Buddha said, in the Sutta-Nipata:

Just as with her own life
a mother shields from hurt
her own, her only child,

let all-embracing thought
for all that lives be thine,

an all-embracing love
for all the universe
in all its heights and depths
and breadth, unstinted love,
unmarred by hate within,
not rousing enmity.[9]

As we look around the postmodern world, we must wonder how its confusing shape would change if more people took seriously the ancient, outmoded and "dead" narratives that sustained our ancestors in ages past. What would happen if more people—logical arguments and postmodernist theory notwithstanding—decided to take seriously the message of the ages in contemporary times?

We live in an age of darkness that is paradoxically also an age of light, an age of exciting and massive transition that in one sense is unprecedented but that, in the end, will undoubtedly be seen to be the same as human life has always been, precariously caught between

---

[8]Ibid., p. 51.

[9]*Teachings of the Compassionate Buddha,* E. A. Burtt, ed. New York: Mentor, 1955. p. 47.

mystery and knowledge, trying to give voice in the darkness to what it perceives to be light.

There will never be a Utopia. The name itself means "no place," but we may at least be able to live our way out of our current "dystopia."* We can at least, as individuals, change ourselves into creatures who put love before hate, tantalizing questions before too easy answers.

That seems so little sometimes in the face of the enormous problems we face today, and yet the most profound minds of the species say it is enough. "It is like a mustard seed which at the time of its sowing in the soil is the smallest of all the seeds on earth; yet once it is sown it grows into the biggest shrub of them all and puts out big branches so that the birds of the air can shelter in its shade." (Mark 4:31-2)

Those who can rise to a higher, yet very ancient consciousness in the midst of the current confusion can act like a yeast or ferment in the world, raising the rest of the postmodern world with them. This will not be easy to do, given the tenor of the times, but then it never was. The Upanishads advise us, "The path is narrow and difficult to tread as the edge of a razor."

And yet, what we are charged with, in this bleak dehumanizing time, is optimism in the midst of a desperate situation. As Kierkegaard wrote one hundred years ago, nothing else matters really.

> ". . . eternity asks of thee and of every individual among these million millions only one question, whether thou hast lived in despair or not, whether thou wast in despair in such a way that thou didst not know thou wast in despair, or in such a way that thou didst hiddenly carry this sickness in thine inward parts as thy gnawing secret, carry it under thy heart as the fruit of a sinful love, or in such a way that thou, a horror to others, didst rave in despair. And if so, if thou hast lived in despair (whether for the rest thou didst win or lose), then for thee all is lost, eternity knows thee not, it never knew thee, or (even more dreadful) it knows thee as thou art known, it puts thee under arrest by thyself in despair."[10]

---

[10]Soren Kierkegaard, *Fear and Trembling and the Sickness Unto Death*. Walter Lowrie, tr. Princeton: Princeton Univ. Press, 1941. pp. 160-61.

Throughout this essay, we have been developing the metaphor of the map, attempting to trace a sort of spiritual geography of the modern and post-modern world. In that metaphor, we have used the idea that the world's religions and mythologies—as well as the myth-making capacity in contemporary human beings—are all maps, guides to the land we hope to traverse. There is always a danger in this business that one can begin to confuse the metaphor with what it describes, to take the map for the landscape it represents. Mapmaking and map reading are complicated businesses. In order to be successful, you must be sophisticated enough to understand that the lines and the squiggles on the surface of the paper are mere representations of a landscape which in reality has little resemblance to the page one is looking at. You must know that highways are not blue and red lines, that bridges are not inverted parentheses, that marshes are not little x's drawn neatly, that holding a map in your hand is not traveling the highway or reaching the destination.

I recently purchased a replica of a map of North America used by early French explorers in the 1600's. It is, by modern standards of cartography, primitive. The land and water masses sketched on it are crude representations of the real shapes of the Great Lakes and the lands around them. Yet, for its time, it was state of the art and, for the explorers of the New World, it was indispensable.

If, however, later explorers had not refined their maps of the region, if generations of surveyors had not plodded through the swamps and woodlands, braving mosquitoes and deer flies to plot out the land, our knowledge of the shape of where we are would have remained primitive.

Spiritually, I believe, we are in the position of those early cartographers, the first to reach what they called The New World. Gradually, a picture of the world they had "discovered" emerged until its actual extent and shape were known.

We, too, stand at the edge of the brave new continent. After the past centuries of "progress" we seem to have found ourselves in the middle of a dark forest with no stars, no discernible landmarks to guide us or locate us in space or time with any accuracy.

And yet, we, like explorers before us, have the work of previous cartographers to guide us, even if their maps no longer describe the landscape in which we find ourselves.

We are in desperate need of new maps for the future.

At the edges of old maps, where the known territory ran out, the ancient cartographers wrote *terra incognita* and "Here there be dragons." For the timid, this was reason to avoid those places, but for those who wished to push themselves and their society forward, the challenge of dragons and unknown territory was all the more reason to go.

As Joseph Campbell knew, even the most adventurous of us do not travel without companions:

> . . . for the heroes of all time have gone before us. The labyrinth is thoroughly known; we have only to follow the thread of the hero path. And where we had thought to find an abomination, we shall find a god. And where we had thought to slay another, we shall slay ourselves. And where we had thought to travel outward, we shall come to the center of our own existence. And where we had thought to be alone, we shall be with all the world.[11]

---

[11] Joseph Campbell with Bill Moyers, *The Power of Myth*. New York: Doubleday, 1988. p. 123.

Glossary

Agnostic
> Term coined in the nineteenth century by T. H. Huxley for someone who would not believe in God or other spiritual realities without positive scientific proof.

Anthropomorphic
> Human form.

Apotheosize
> To make divine.

Archetypes
> Jung's term for the deep forms or psychological models that inhabit the unconscious. These archetypes are universal (e.g. the idea of the divine mother) but manifest themselves differently in various cultures (e.g. Parvati in Hinduism, the Blessed Virgin Mary in Catholicism). These surface forms that the archetypes take manifest themselves individually in dreams and collectively as the symbols found in world religions.

Asanas
> The various positions or postures of *hatha yoga*.

Autonomic nervous system
> The collective term for the system which regulates those functions of the body, such as heartbeat, digestion, respiration, the flight-fight response, etc., which lie largely below the threshold of conscious control.

Axial Age

> The period from about 1,000 B.C. to about 1,000 A.D. when all the current major world religions came on the scene.

Cogito

> The "thinker" or subject in Descartes' philosophy.

Commissurotomy

> An operation which severs any commissure, or juncture between anatomical parts, including severing the *corpus collossum* which normally links the left and right hemispheres of the brain.

Conscious mind

> That part of the mind which is focused, rational and more or less aware of its own working. (See also Unconscious mind.)

Cosmos

> The universe as an organized, ordered and harmonic system, the opposite of chaos.

Creationism

> A modern Bible-based alternative to the Theory of Evolution which attempts to reconcile some scientific findings with the Creation story in Genesis.

Cybernetic

> Concerned with communication and control, especially through automatic or electrical-mechanical systems.

Dreamtime, the Dreaming

> In Australian aboriginal mythology, the time of the creation of the world, the time of origins. (See also the Songlines.)

Drive behavior / Drive mechanism

> A repeated behavior pattern (e.g. chanting) that induces changes in psychological states (e.g. ritual trance).

Dystopia

> A state of mind and being characterized by confusion, anxiety and the sense of a lack of order.

Edge City

Term coined by journalist Joel Garreau for suburban developments being built on the traditional edges of older cities. Usually clustered around freeway interchanges, their most striking feature is their linear commercial strip of shopping malls, drive-through restaurants, etc.

Elementargedanken

Adolph Bastian's term for universal ideas found in all or almost all human societies. (See also Archetypes.) These "elementary ideas" express themselves in various forms in various cultures. Bastian called the local manifestations of these deep forms *Volksgedanken.*

Entraining

Bringing bodily and mental systems into synchronization by forming neurological pathways that tend towards a more holistic experience.

Ergotropic system

The physiological system which tends towards greater excitement. (See Tropotropic system.)

Ethology/ethologists

The study of behavior in animals and humans and the scientists who study that behavior.

Evolution

The scientific theory, first fully articulated by Charles Darwin in 1859, that forms of life change into other forms through the process of Natural Selection. (See also Natural Selection.)

Exogamy

Marriage outside the tribe or clan group.

Gestalt

A whole pattern, an integrated configuration against which individual features may stand out.

Great Chain of Being

The idea, popular in the Middle Ages and Renaissance, that the existence of all beings is linked in a hierarchical and interdependent system.

Hierarchical

Ordered from high to low or from simple to complex with clear distinctions between levels.

Homeostasis / homeostatic

A state of equilibrium or balance among bodily systems.

Hybris

A Greek term for overbearing pride, we might say ego-inflation, which leads to the downfall of tragic heroes in Greek tragedies.

Intertextuality

(See Postmodern/postmodernism.)

Labyrinth

A complex spatial pattern similar to a maze which may differ from a maze in the absence of blind alleys, dead ends, etc. The spiral pattern of a labyrinth may be followed directly from its entrance to its center.

Libido

In psychodynamic theory, libido is the flow of psychic energy through the individual. In Freud's terms, this flow was primarily directed towards sexuality while in Jung's terminology, it is more broad based in its aims and focus.

Limbic system

(See Old mammalian brain.)

Liminal

A threshold state, between states, especially in ritual.

Luddism

A late eighteenth and early nineteenth century labor movement which attempted to forestall or reverse the Industrial Revolution through sabotage of machinery.

Macrocosm
> The "large universe," or cosmos, the context within which all happens.

Mammalian Brain
> (See New Mammalian Brian.)

Microcosm
> The "small universe," or individual human being, which is a mirror image of the "large universe," the macrocosm.

Modern / modernism
> Though the word "modern" usually means whatever is happening "now," in this book it is used to denote the complex of technological, social and cultural changes that took place between about 1880 and the early 1970's. These changes led generally to an increased pace of living, greater fragmentation of ideas, artistic forms, and values, and greater alienation of people from one another, their environment, and their own past. When used to define artistic movements, "modern" usually denotes the period from about the late 1800's (Impressionism, Expressionism) through such "modern" movements as Cubism, Surrealism, Minimalism, etc., through the early 1970's. In architecture, it would include the International Style and Bauhaus. (See Postmodern/postmodernism.)

Mystical participation
> That state of mind, most commonly found among primal peoples, in which one experiences a sense of identification with a much larger life, sometimes identified as the life of the cosmos itself. It is this sense of mystical participation that makes such things as totemism possible, where one's individual existence is intimately bound up with that of another being, the totem animal. In this state, the usual distinction we make between the sacred and the profane is abolished.

Mythos
> A body of sacred stories.

Narrative

Essentially "story," but this includes not only stories as such, but all modes of expression that depend on story or narrative for their significance, including painting, dance, music, etc.

Natural Selection

The mechanism, in Darwin's theory of Evolution, by which Nature selects desirable traits to be passed on to succeeding generations.

Neocortex

The forebrain of humans, seat of such higher mental functions as speech, rational thought, etc. Also called, by P. D. MacLean, the new mammalian brain. (See also Triune Brain.)

Neurasthenia

A physical and psychological state characterized by fatigue, depression, hypersensitivity, etc.

New mammalian brain

(See Neocortex.)

Noumena / noumenal

Kant's term for the unknowable realm beyond the phenomena we can perceive. (See Phenomena.)

Old mammalian brain

In MacLean's triune brain, the structures included in this level of the human brain are shared with other mammals, especially the higher primates, and include such functions as territoriality, aggression, procreational urges, etc. (See also Triune Brain.)

Old Reptilian Brain

(See Reptilian Brain.)

Ontological

Having to do with the nature of existence and with relationships among things which exist.

Paradigm

An intellectual framework or model of how the universe, or some portion of it works. In astronomy, for example, the system of Ptolemy (sun goes around the earth) makes up one paradigm, that of Copernicus (earth goes around the sun) is another paradigm. Calculations made or conclusions reached in one paradigm are meaningless in another. The principles of Freudian psychoanalysis, the assumptions of Marxism, and the postulates of Euclidian geometry are examples of other paradigms or systems of thought.

Parousia

In Christian mythology, the Second Coming of Jesus at the end of time when all things will be brought to fulfillment.

Participation mystique

(See Mystical participation.)

Phenomena / phenomenal

The visible world, accessible through the senses.

Platonic

Ideal, derived from the Greek philosopher Plato's philosophy.

Postmodern / postmodernism

A philosophic, artistic and critical attitude which has developed since the 1970's, primarily influenced by such French writers as Jean-Francois Lyotard, Jacques Derrida, Michel Foucault, Roland Barthes, and others which emphasizes the uncertainty of knowledge and criticism. Ideas, artistic forms, philosophies and knowledge have meaning and validity only within the bounds of intellectual paradigms. (See Paradigms.) Thus, the meaning of any given text, idea or bit of information is constantly in flux and no one meaning or interpretation has any "privilege" over any other. All is the interplay of competing texts ("intertextuality") which vie with each other for acceptance. Thus, the term is used to describe an attitude towards knowledge and even the ability to know things more than to denote a particular period of history or organized school of thought.

Primum mobile

The "first mover" of the universe which provides the motive force for all the planets, stars, and life itself.

Progress

> The nineteenth- and twentieth-century notion that each period of history is built upon the achievements of previous periods in an open-ended process of betterment. Improvement was usually measured in terms of material prosperity and technological refinements. Postmodernists would argue against this idea of progress, saying only that one historical paradigm replaces another without implying any necessary "advancement" over previous periods or paradigms.

Psychoanalytic theory

> The model of the mind and personality put forth around the turn of the twentieth century by Sigmund Freud which divided the psyche into conscious and unconscious realms.

Reptilian brain

> MacLean's term for the deepest and most primitive level of the human brain, responsible for basic survival functions. (See also Triune Brain.)

Ritual

> A series of repeated actions or words which have the intention and effect of blurring the usual boundary between the sacred and the profane.

Sacred

> Of or belonging to the realm of the divine, spiritual, or transcendent, usually seen as in opposition to "the profane" or secular. (See Secular.)

Salvation history

> In Christian belief, the unified story of mankind's fall from innocence in the Garden of Eden, its redemption by Jesus and its eventual union with God after the Final Judgment.

Science / scientific thought

> A method of acquiring knowledge about the physical world that originated with the ancient Greeks but that was fully developed only since about 1650 A.D. The scientific method relies on observation of physical phenomena and making

logical deductions from observations. Its results are generally quantifiable (i.e. capable of being expressed in numbers.)

Secular

Of or belonging to the realm of the non-spiritual, the opposite or complement of "sacred." (See Sacred.)

Secular materialist culture

A society whose norms and values are largely based on non-spiritual, material standards such as money, quantity, etc. Questions of the spirit or religion rarely come up in daily life and are distinctly separated from such areas as public policy, government and public education.

Skepticism

An attitude of doubt as to the certainty of any knowledge.

Songlines

The "dreaming tracks" of Australian aborigines. The Songlines, learned from youth, form a sort of spiritual and geographic map of Australia for the aborigines.

Structuralism

A branch of anthropology which sees social customs, rituals, taboos, etc., as more or less arbitrary forms which bind societies together.

Stupa

A mound or tower forming part of a Buddhist or Hindu shrine.

Systematic doubt

Descartes' method of stripping away all the ideas and mental impressions he had of which he could not be absolutely certain. His goal was to lay a solid foundation for his philosophy.

Terra incognita

"Unknown land," a term used to mark unknown territories on ancient maps.

Theriomorphic

Animal form.

Topography

> The physical layout of a landscape, including both its natural and manmade features and the interrelationship of these features.

Transcendent

> Going beyond the merely physical.

Triune brain

> P. D. MacLean's term for the total human brain which consists of the reptilian, the old mammalian and the new mammalian brains. (See Old mammalian brain, Neocortex, and Reptilian brain.)

Tropotropic system

> The physiological system which tends towards greater relaxation. (See Ergotropic system.)

Unconscious mind

> That part of the psyche of which we are largely unaware but which manifests itself in dreams, daydreams, fantasies, etc. In Jungian analytical psychology, it is the region of the archetypes. (See also Conscious mind.)

Upanishads

> Hindu sacred scriptures and philosophical works.

Virtuosi

> The name given to the early practioners of the scientific method, especially the English scientists of the seventeenth century.

Western / western civilization

> The complex of historical events, social patterns, ideas and artistic forms from the ancient Greeks to modern times that gave rise to the European (and European descended) cultures.

World center

> Also known as an *axis mundi*, the world center is an imaginary point believed to be the center of the earth, the meeting place of the upper, middle and lower worlds.

World picture/worldview

> The mental image of the world that we carry in our heads which forms the expectations and basic operating assumptions of our lives that we rarely question because they seem so obvious. Similar to paradigms but more inclusive in that a worldview is not merely an intellectual construct but includes emotions, irrational beliefs, mythologies, etc. (See Paradigms.)

Zeitgeist

> A German term which means "spirit of the times." The term is used to designate the prevailing feeling or mood of a particular culture and period of history.

Zen

> Branch of Buddhism which emphasizes direct transmission of the spirit of Buddhism outside scriptures rather than inculcation of doctrine through scriptures.

Ziggurat

> A stepped pyramid of the sort found in ancient Mesopotamia.

Suggestions for Further Discussion or Reflection

[The following suggestions may be helpful to instructors who wish to use this book as a spur to further discussion or to individual readers who may want suggestions for further individual reflection on the ideas presented in *The Geography of Nowhere*. Suggestions for further reading are included for those who may wish to explore individual areas in greater detail.]

Chapter One

1. Use your imagination to reverse the time travel of our guest from 1845. What changes would you be most likely to notice if you went back in time to a previous era? What would be missing from your life? Would life be easier, harder or just different? What would you miss most? Would you choose to stay in that time? Why? What would the trade-offs be if you could live in a different period of history? What do these reflections tell you about your own values?

2. Most of the technological and social changes that we call "modern" seem to have been motivated by the values of speed, efficiency and ease. Are there situations in our lives when slowness, inefficiency and difficulty might be more desirable values? Give examples.

3. Select a modern invention such as television, radio, the fax machine and discuss whether it contributes to a greater sense of fragmentation and alienation or to a feeling of wholeness and community. In the case of radio, television or computer net-

works, how do these inventions change the very definition of "community" as we have traditionally used that word?

4. Discuss in what ways you have experienced the relativism and apathetic attitude ("too hip to care") of the postmodern world. Why do so many people today seem to adopt this attitude? Are they simply overwhelmed by the amount of information reaching them? Are they seeking to avoid pain by it? To what extent is your own worldview affected by it?

5. Give some examples of contemporary people who do care about and who are involved in finding solutions for the problems of our times. Do we generally regard these people as realists or hopeless idealists?

6. Examine some contemporary works of art (paintings, poems, songs, sculpture) and discuss the images of being human that are presented in them. Is the vision hopeful, optimistic? Compare contemporary images with images from other periods of history and/or other cultures. What do you conclude about the values of these various cultures?

For Further Reading

Eliade, Mircea. *Myths, Dreams and Mysteries: the Encounter Between Contemporary Faiths and Archaic Realities.* New York: Harper Torchbooks. 1967.

Garreau, Joel. *Edge City: Life on the New Frontier.* New York: Doubleday. 1991.

Lyotard, Jean-Francois. *The Postmodernism Condition: A Report on Knowledge.* Geoff Bennington and Brian Massumi, tr. Minneapolis: University of Minnesota Press. 1984.

Marshall, Brenda K. *Teaching the Postmodern: Fiction and Theory.* New York: Routledge. 1992.

Meyrowitz, Joshua. *No Sense of Place: The Impact of Electronic Media On Social Behavior.* New York: Oxford Univ. Press. 1984.

Chapter Two

1. Examine the architecture of a contemporary church. In what ways is it similar to the architecture of older sacred places such as Gothic cathedrals or ancient Buddhist temples as discussed in this chapter? How is the church constructed to form a "world center" as described in this chapter?

2. Compare an older section of your city (a neighborhood built before 1940) and a more modern section (a recent subdivision with a nearby strip mall). Economics aside, what differences would you expect to experience if you lived in either of these two areas? Would the physical organization of one (its "topography") tend towards more or less interaction with neighbors? What differences would you find in a neighborhood where people walked instead of drove? Where neighborhood social life focused on the front porch instead of the backyard? What are some of the *social* implications of the way we lay out the places where we live?

3. Describe experiences you have had (e.g. walking along a beach, climbing a mountain) where the separation between yourself and the world and some "divine" power seemed not to exist. What was the experience like? How did it feel? How did it change the way you looked at the world? Was the change permament or temporary? Why?

4. Examine your family's holiday customs (e.g. Easter Egg hunt, Thanksgiving dinner). In what ways do these customs or "rituals" give your family life a center and focus that it does not seem to have at non-holiday times? How would it feel *not* to have them one year?

For Further Reading

Campbell, Joseph. *The Way of the Seeded Earth.* New York: Harper and Row. 1988.

Eliade, Mircea. *Cosmos and History: The Myth of the Eternal Return.* New York: Harper Torchbooks. 1959.

von Simpson, Otto. *The Gothic Cathedral.* Princeton: Princeton Univ. Press. 1988.

Zimmer, Heinrich. *Artistic Form and the Sacred Images of India.* Princeton: Princeton Univ. Press. 1984.

Chapter Three

1. Compare the view of the physical universe discussed in this chapter (the Great Chain of Being, etc.) with our contemporary view of the universe and what we know about it. What would living in the older sort of universe "feel" like? How would it change your concept of what it means to be a human being?

2. How would the style of writing of the Renaissance scientists, with its many references to God, be received by the contemporary scientific community? Do you think contemporary scientists share the goals of the *virtuosi* to find God's order in the physical universe? Would a belief in a divinely ordered universe help or hinder a scientist in his/her work today or wouldn't it make any difference?

3. In what ways have modern science and technology exhibited *hybris*? Do you feel that in some areas (e.g. genetic engineering) scientists are tempted to "play God"?

For Further Reading

Russell, Bertrand. *The Wisdom of the West.* New York: Crescent Books. 1969.

Tillyard, E. M. W. *The Elizabethan World Picture.* New York: Vintage Books. n.d.

Westfall, Richard S. *Science and Religion in Seventeenth Century England.* Ann Arbor: Ann Arbor Paperbacks. 1972.

Chapter Four

1. Using Descartes' method of systematic doubt, explore your own beliefs and conception of the world. What are the sources of your worldview? Where did you get your ideas about how the world works? Which of your beliefs would you consider "unshakable"? Why?

2. Is the scientific worldview as it has developed over the past several hundred years really incompatible with a religious worldview? Why? Why not? Do you have to "compartmentalize" your beliefs, keeping your knowledge about the world separate from your beliefs?

3. What is the difference between "knowing" and "believing"? Is "religion" simply the word we use for the things we don't know?

4. Is there a difference between "religion" and "spirituality"? Can a person have one without the other.

5. Read the description of the creation of the world in Genesis. Compare it with creation myths from other cultures. Compare all these sacred cosmogonies with what you know about biological evolution and the Big Bang theory of the universe's origins. Do you think scientists and religionists are speaking two separate languages? If so, which language should we believe? Or should we learn to be "bilingual"?

For Further Reading

Barrett, William. *Death of the Soul: From Descartes to the Computers*. Garden City: Anchor Books. 1987.

Irvine, William. *Apes, Angels and Victorians*. New York: Time Inc. 1963.

Chapter Five

1. Do you think the analogy made in this chapter between the primitive needs of the human body and the ancient needs of the human spirit is a valid one? If so, in what ways does our society encourage or discourage us from fulfilling these needs? Is fulfilling these needs helped or hindered by our typical modern lifestyle? What changes could you make in your personal lifestyle to further your spiritual growth?

2. Use a dream journal to explore your dreams. Keep a pad of paper and a pencil by your bedside and record your dreams on waking. Observe in particular the way time and space operate in your dreams. What do you make of the apparent "fluidity" of

time and space in dreams? How is this similar to what happens
in stories drawn from mythology?

3. "Mana" is a term from Polynesian mythology which means the
ineffable power of the universe that one experiences from time to
time in moments of sacred vision. Have you ever experienced
"mana," an overwhelming force over which you had no control?
What was it like?

For Further Reading

Dubos, Rene. *Celebrations of Life*. New York: McGraw Hill. 1981.

Eliade, Mircea. *Cosmos and History: The Myth of the Eternal Return*.
New York: Harper Torchbooks. 1959.

—. *Myth and Reality*. New York: Harper Torchbooks. 1963.

—. *Myths, Dreams and Mysteries: the Encounter Between Contemporary Faiths and Archaic Realities*. New York: Harper
Torchbooks. 1960.

Jung, Carl G. *Man and His Symbols*. New York: Doubleday. 1964.

Stevens, Anthony. *Archetypes: A Natural History of the Self*. New
York: Quill. 1983.

—. *On Jung*. New York: Routledge. 1990.

—. *The Two Million Year Old Self*. College Station, TX: Texas
A&M University Press. 1993.

Chapter Six

1. Describe what, if any, symbols have intense significance for you
(e.g. the flag, the cross, your local or school football mascot).
How would you describe the feeling you get when you see these
things? Is there a simple one-to-one correspondence between the
symbols in your life and what they mean to you. Does the flag,
for example, simply mean "patriotism" or is there more to it?
Based on MacLean's model of the triune brain, why do you think
it is so difficult to put into words what symbols mean?

2. Learn a poem or song you like "by heart." Recite or sing the
piece with feeling. How is the experience different from simply

reading the poem from a book or singing the song from a score? When you memorize something, how do you do it? What is the *process* by which you remember all the words and notes? Is this different from memorizing strings of facts for a test?

3. What personal landmarks do you use to locate yourself in space? After a long trip, how do you know when you are coming "home"? What different meanings do these landscape features have? Do you associate them with stories or personal history?

For Further Reading

Barrett, William. *The Illusion of Technique.* New York: Anchor Books. 1979.

Chatwin, Bruce. *The Songlines.* New York: Penguin. 1987.

Fox, Robin. *The Search for Society: Quest for a Biological Science and Morality.* New Brunswick, NJ: Rutgers Univ. Press. 1969.

Hillman, James. *Healing Fiction.* Barrytown, NY: Station Hill. 1983.

MacLean, P. D. *The Triune Concept of Brain and Behavior.* T. J. Boag and D. Campbell, eds. Toronto: Univ. of Toronto Press. 1973.

Chapter Seven

1. Chant a single syllable repeatedly, clap rhythmically or practice a repeated rhythmic movement for ten to fifteen minutes. What changes do you experience in your normal physiological and psychological state? Based on the studies cited in this chapter, what is happening to your ergotropic and tropotropic systems?

2. Sit straight in a chair or in a meditation posture for fifteen or twenty minutes without moving. Try to breathe rhythmically without forcing your breath. Simply concentrate on relaxing the body muscle by muscle, focusing on the easy flow of breath in and out of your lungs. At the end of the period, describe how you feel. How do these feelings differ from your normal feelings and awareness? How are they similar to or different from the feelings you experienced in number 1 above.

3. Listen to examples of "sacred" music such as Buddhist chanting, Gregorian chant, African tribal chanting, etc. What similarities are there among these different styles of music? In what way might they all have the same goal in mind?

4. What would it be like to belong to a religious tradition where the main form of religious expression is the dance rather than the spoken, or read, word?

5. In what sense is the view of the world as presented by Science also a "mythology," i.e. a story which connects together the separated experiences and phenomena of life? (What is the "story" implicit in the Big Bang Theory, for example, or in Darwin's Theory of Evolution?)

For Further Reading

D'Aquili, Eugene and Charles Laughlin. *The Spectrum of Ritual: A Biogenetic Structural Analysis.* New York: Columbia Univ. Press. 1979.

Turner, Victor. *The Ritual Process: Structure and Anti-structure.* New York: Cornell Univ. Press. 1977.

Chapter Eight

1. Write an original poem, choreograph and perform a dance, write and sing a song, create a painting or sculpture which expresses your deepest feelings about who you are and how you are related to the universe you find yourself in.

2. Find a myth or story from some other religious tradition than your own and compare it with one from your own religious tradition. How do these other stories shed light on your own religious experience, help you to get new ideas, or to break mental and spiritual gridlock and get fresh perspectives on old beliefs?

3. Spend time by yourself without background music, TV, books, etc. Maybe you could take a long walk in the woods or just spend some time alone. What does being alone reveal about yourself? Did you find the time alone boring, challenging, re-

vealing, frightening, valuable? Why? What new insights about yourself were you able to take away from the experience?

4. Find others of like mind, who share your concerns and attitudes, and start a prayer or study group to continue to explore appropriate forms for expressing spirituality in the postmodern world.

For Further Reading

Berry, Philippa and Andrew Wernick, eds. *Shadow of Spirit: Postmodernism and Religion.* New York: Routledge. 1992.

Campbell, Joseph. *The Hero with a Thousand Faces.* Princeton: Princeton Univ. Press. 1972.

—-. *The Masks of God.* New York: Penguin. 1969.

Capra, Fritjof. *The Tao of Physics.* New York: Bantam. 1983.

Ferris, Timothy. *Coming of Age in the Milky Way.* New York: Wm. Morrow and Co. 1988.

Gleick, James. *Chaos: Making a New Science.* New York: Viking. 1987.

Hawking, Stephen W. *A Brief History of Time.* Toronto: Bantam. 1988.

Smith, Huston. *Beyond the Post-modern Mind.* Wheaton, IL: Theosophical Society. 1991.

Index